Porphyria

Porphyria

The Woman Who Has
"The Vampire Disease"

Tammy Evans

New Horizon Press   Far Hills, NJ

Requests for permission should be addressed to:
New Horizon Press
P.O. Box 669
Far Hills, NJ 07931

Evans, Tammy
    Porphyria
    The Woman Who Has "The Vampire Disease"

Library of Congress Catalog Card Number: Pending

ISBN: 0-88282-156-3

Interior Layout: Howard Simpson

New Horizon Press

Manufactured in the U.S.A.

2001 2000 1999 1998 1997 / 5 4 3 2 1

*To my dear husband, Tim and my four
beautiful children, Lori, Dan, Johanna
and Reuben. Thank you for your
unconditional love and undying patience.*

*To Sharon Bruce. Thank you for
encouraging me.*

To my Mother. I love you.

*"Out of suffering have emerged the strongest souls; the
most massive
characters are seared with scars."*
— *E. H. Chapin*

*Nor could to-night's gay feast restrain
A sudden thought of one so pale
For love of her, and all in vain:
So, she was come through wind and rain.*

Porphyria's Lover

Robert Browning

Contents

Author's Note

These are my actual experiences and history, and this book reflects my opinion of the past, present, and future. The personalities, events, actions, and conversations portrayed within the story have been reconstructed from my memory and research, utilizing documents, press accounts, and the memories of participants. In an effort to safeguard the privacy of certain individuals, I have changed their names and in some cases, altered otherwise identifying characteristics and locations. Events involving the characters happened as described.

Chapter 1

A Glimpse of Darkness

"What's wrong with Mommy?" I half-whispered to Grandma, my daddy's mother, as she made her way through our dimly lit house. At five I had to take double steps to keep up with her. "Why won't Mommy come out of the bedroom? Why is the house so dark? Why are the drapes closed again?"

"Shh!" Grandma said, putting one of her exquisitely manicured pink nails over my mouth.

"But. . . ."

"Shh!" she said again more insistently, "Your mom is very sick."

"You can help her get well, Grandma. You always do a good job of making me better when I don't feel good."

Tears started to roll down her cheeks. "This is a different kind of sickness, baby girl. Grandma doesn't know how to make this kind go away," she said.

A frightening sensation came over me. I was confused. How could there be certain kinds of sicknesses that Grandma didn't know how to make better? But then, I remembered...

My other grandpa, Mommy's father, got one of those

kind. My "old" Grandma was sick like that, too. Mommy told me about how she visited "old" Grandma at the hospital where people acted funny. That grandma is in heaven now. Grandpa is there, too. The doctors and nurses didn't know how to make them better. That's what Mommy said. She said they had a sickness there wasn't any medicine for. Did Mommy have that same kind of sickness? It was one, she had said, that a lot of people in her family got.

My heart began to pound very hard and fast.

"Grandma!" I called out, gripped by realization. My sobs began and my body trembled. "Does Mommy have the same kind of sickness Grandpa and old Grandma had?"

"Oh dear God!" Grandma knelt down and pulled me close to her. She held onto me for a long time.

So Grandma knows about the sickness. . . . Sometimes, when the grownups think I'm asleep in my bed, they talk quietly in the other room about it. They call it "poor fear." I've never heard of a sickness like that before. Mommy cries a lot when they talk about it. I heard her tell Daddy that she's afraid that I'll get it someday, too. When she talks about that, Daddy gets mad and stomps out the door. Maybe that's why she cries. I don't know, but Grandma does. Whatever it is, it is bad, so bad Grandma can't fix it.

I had never felt so frightened. We held onto each other until the tears were all cried out. Then Grandma said, "You stay here. I need to talk to your mommy."

I stamped my feet. "I do, too. Why can't I go in the room? It's stupid."

"Yes, it's stupid, Tammy. I have to agree with you on that one. Nevertheless, that's what your mommy wants and we'll have to abide by it." She pulled back the cuff of her sleeve and noted the time on her watch. "All right, it's almost three o'clock. Here's my watch. I'll be back in fifteen minutes."

I held the watch tightly in my hand and saw where the minute hand was. She opened the door only a little, went in, and closed it again. I heard the lock click. I stood like a statue for the longest time. Finally Grandma came back out.

"Tammy, go outside and around to the back window. Your mom is going to open the curtains and say hello so you'll see she's okay. And Tammy, don't let her see you cry. That will only make her sadder."

"When will she come?"

"Very soon, Tammy. It's just going to take her a few minutes to walk there because she's very weak and tired." Grandma was smiling now.

I ran out of the house and around the back, over to the window whose curtains were still drawn. Slowly they opened only two inches or so. Then, as if in slow motion, a frail hunched-over form appeared, supported by Grandma. Even though the room behind her was dark, I could make out that Mommy's face was swollen, covered with red blotches, and she was wearing a pair of black sunglasses over her eyes. But the disguise could not hide her from me. She was still my beautiful mommy, and she was coming to the window. I would finally be nearer to her.

"Hi, Mommy!" I yelled. I jumped up and down, desperate to get closer. "Can you hear me?"

She waved back weakly and nodded her head. Grandma held onto her body as Mommy leaned against the window to get closer to me.

"Mommy," I shouted, "Your lips are moving, but I

can't hear what you're saying."

Mommy mouthed words over and over, then she slipped away from the light. Grandma opened the window and called loud enough for me to hear, "She's trying to say she loves you, Tammy." Then she shut it again.

I felt like crying because Mommy was trying so hard to say words loud enough for me to hear, but she didn't have the strength. Then I remembered Grandma telling me not to cry. I swallowed the lump in my throat that kept trying to come out along with the tears behind my eyes. *If Mommy is going to get better, she'll need to see only smiles.* I stood on the tiptoes of my shiny patent leather buckle shoes and smiled the biggest smile I could. Waving to her as hard and fast as I could, I screamed the loudest I have ever screamed in my life, "I LOVE YOU, MOMMY!!!"

Then I thought of the conversation I'd overheard the night before.

Maybe that's why Mommy's crying. Maybe that's why they call it "poor fear."

It was not long after my mother's attack that my parents divorced. I was six. My father dropped out of my life and my mother remarried.

We lived in California until, without warning, the manufacturing plant where my stepfather was employed as a supervisor closed. Our life suddenly changed. When she wasn't ill my mother worked as an accountant for a CPA firm in Sacramento, but it wasn't enough to keep our family going. Despite months of searching, my stepfather was unable to find another job. Out of money and painfully close to losing our home, my parents made the only choice they could. We sold everything and moved to Alpena, Michigan, where my grandparents lived. There were jobs there. With her accounting skills, even though her illness caused frequent absences, Mom quickly found work. Dad, with his engineering experience, also found a good position.

It was late December before we got settled. At first I thought Alpena had the appearance of a barren wasteland with its deep snow and unclothed timbers that only slightly resembled what I knew as trees. The sky was dull and mournful, at least so I thought until I realized that this lack of light might help my mother who would not have to go out in the sun wrapped like an Egyptian mummy.

Although my brother, Dan, and I felt sad about moving and having to attend a new school, we tried to make the best of it and find new friends.

One day I invited a few classmates home. Unfortunately, unbeknownst to me, Mommy had suffered a bad attack that morning. Not wanting to cancel my first social plans, she pulled her aching body from bed, baked chocolate chip cookies and set out cups of juice, then waited for us, knowing that the other children's parents would expect her to be there. From the street we could see her standing at the door, her hair covered by a large black scarf and huge dark glasses over her eyes. I knew why and shuddered. As we got closer, she opened the door and ushered us in. Inside the house all the drapes had been tightly shut. The girls looked kind of shocked, but I was grateful no one spoke about it. Still, I could see how ill at ease they were. Soon they called one of the mothers to come and get them.

The next morning my stepfather, who adored me and whom I had come to think of as "daddy," drove me to school.

Getting out of the car I saw my visitors from the day before pointing at me. Thinking they wanted to talk to me, I walked towards them. They were singing a rhyme. As I got closer I could make out the words.

> Tammy, Tammy, skin so white,
> You're a creature of the night.
> Seeing your face is pretty scary,
> But your mom's is downright eerie.

Tears rolling down my cheeks, I ran inside the school. For the rest of the day, whenever a kid got near me, he or she would hum that tune or mouth the words. Never again did I invite children home.

Chapter 2

Hungry for Love

"Dad! Dad, come quick!" In my head it sounded as if I was screaming for help, but in reality muffled whispers alone fell from my lips, curled in an anguished expression. He couldn't possibly hear me. . . .

Mom, where are you! My thoughts begged her to come help me, but I could not give them voice.

Terribly weak, I toppled onto the bathroom floor, crawled to the toilet and inched my way up so I could hang my head over the bowl. The need to vomit intensified, but all that came up was a ferocious sequence of dry heaves. Over and over I retched. Then, painful waves of cramping from my lower intestines began: my body wanted to purge itself but could not. Another pain, very sharp and intense in my lower right side doubled my body over and threw me violently to the floor. It felt like someone was punching me in the same sore spot over and over again. My heart pounded loudly, hard and fast, as if it were going to jump right out of my chest! I stood up but was overcome by another wave of nausea. Then the bathroom started spinning.

The thud of my head hitting the wall as I fell brought my stepfather and mother running. "Call an ambulance!" my mother screamed.

At the hospital, the doctor told my parents, "It looks like an appendicitis attack. Her appendix will have to be removed immediately."

My dry heaves had ended and now a sharp pain stung my side. Although my heart was beating at an alarming rate, the doctor politely suggested it was because I was upset and scared. "No need to worry. It will be a routine two-hour operation and she can go home in a day or two."

A few hours later, the surgery was performed.

"I'm a bit surprised," the doctor told my stepfather, stripping off his mask. "With the amount of pain your daughter has been experiencing and the accelerated heart rate and abnormalities in the blood test, I expected her appendix to be on the verge of rupturing. Instead, I found it in remarkably good condition. Still, we have every reason to suspect that was the problem. These things can fool you, sealing over sometimes. It's a good thing we removed it."

Forty-eight hours passed.

I was not recovering as expected. My body would not heal. Four days after the operation, pneumonia set in and a staph infection appeared as well.

Late on the day pneumonia set in, as I was being wheeled back from a series of x-rays, I saw a bright yellow sign on my hospital room door. "Isolation." Tears ran down my cheeks. *I don't want to be alone. Why am I being left here?* I could have no visitors other than my parents and a minister. They were allowed to stay for fifteen minutes, once in the morning and once at night.

The pain and fever were enough to drive me out of my mind. Each morning the doctor came in and drained the repulsive smelling infection from the incisions as two nurses held my hands over my head. Antibiotics and fever medication were administered, but neither seemed to improve my condition in any way.

Fear, loneliness, the overpowering medical uncertainty surrounding my future: it was too much for a twelve-year-old girl to handle. With each passing day I became weaker and grew more frightened.

My parents joked that my brother said I looked like I was dead. Although they laughed, it wasn't a very good joke. Despite the insanity of the idea, I became convinced, in my delirium, that my parents were locking me up in this ghastly place to get rid of me. To this fear the mystery surrounding the nature of my condition added ever escalating panic. "Why is this happening?" I cried out when I was alone. I could not rein in my despair and paranoia.

My own strategy for easing the pain was to lie as still as possible. I felt I had to live by my own feeble wits since medicine couldn't seem to help me. My temperature was still up. Now I searched endlessly for a cold spot on the pillow. Then, as chills overcame me, I tried to bunch up the thin blankets and forget. With great effort, I recreated in my thoughts my favorite scene. It was summer and the sun shone down, warming me as I swam in the lake's sparkling aquamarine waters.

In and out of delirium, I lingered like that for weeks. Finally, my mind began to clear and I became a little stronger physically.

On Christmas Eve the doctors agreed that, despite my weakened condition, I should be allowed to go home. I still felt very sick. I was convinced that they were letting me out to die with my family around me, enjoying the last holiday season of my short life.

However, even though I'd lost twenty pounds and couldn't even walk on my own, the comfort of having my mother at my side improved my emotional state incredibly. After a few weeks I was able to study for the first time since my fall in the bathroom. Slowly and tediously, I grew better. By late February, I returned to school, even though I could attend only half-day sessions.

We had all come to believe that my appendix caused this terrible attack and near collapse of my body. As time dragged by and I still complained of feeling sick, my stepfather seemed to blame me for being "unable to throw off the infection." But this, I realized, was his macho way of dealing with the disaster.

It is all over now, we said to ourselves as the summer came upon us. *Life can go on as planned.*

None of us, except perhaps my mother who said nothing, imagined the dark truth behind the puzzling trauma of my childhood illness, or that it would horribly alter the rest of my life.

The rest of my high school years are a blur. Most of the time I kept to myself. Episodes of illness, still strange and never identified, continued. I never tied them to my mother's recurrent attacks and neither did she. Except for my mother's inexplicable silence in regard to her illness, my parents were loving and supportive—perhaps too much so. Now I realize it was to overcompensate for the continued sense of separation I experienced from my high school peers.

September, after my senior year, as I was preparing to go to a nearby college as a day student, the first boy who had ever noticed me sat down beside me on the bus coming home from a youth retreat given by churches across the state. I could hardly believe it. He was tall, blond and handsome, and we began to talk to each other. His attention made me realize how much I'd yearned for love and intimacy. Of course, he did most of the talking and I listened. Throughout the next six months I became so mesmerized by Peter Castle I failed to notice we never hung out with others our age. He seemed impressed that I was always willing to listen to his dreams and share them with him. Somewhere along the way we decided to be married. There was no formal proposal on his part, it just happened, which is the way we envisioned the rest of our lives falling into place. The only formality Peter insisted upon was that I meet his family before the wedding. He had already met mine and seemed to relish their disapproval of him. Perhaps he was hoping the same would be true when I met his folks. Then we truly would be alone together—us against the world.

I met his mother, father, brothers and sisters one Sunday. Peter's parents, Piers and Anna, had immigrated from the Netherlands to the United States in the 1950s to start a new life as school teachers. Most of the Castle relatives were already living in the States and had been encouraging the rest of their family to join them in their prosperity. Peter was the firstborn child. In the traditional Dutch fashion, Piers and Anna created a large family for themselves, eight children in all. The willowy stature and flowing white-blond hair framing the slender bronze faces of Peter's five sisters were startling to me. I felt inferior in their presence. My short stature and "Plain Jane" exterior could never compare with their beauty and grace. But to my surprise, Peter didn't seem to care. Like his brothers, Peter appeared physically perfect; they were all tall blondes with well-defined features. Their piercing blue eyes relayed gentle, yet masculine personalities. Still, there was something about Peter that was distinctly different from the others. As I grew to know his family, I learned that Peter did not adhere to their traditional values. He yearned for something different, something more.

For instance, although they all had a love for the outdoors, Peter had taken it a step further. For several months before we met, he had been living in a self-made lean-to on state forest land. He didn't have steady employment. Instead, Peter lived day-to-day doing odd jobs for cash. Although this was unusual, I found his untamed spirit and enthusiasm wondrous. And the fact that he paid attention to me, miraculous. At the time, I could not (or would not) see Peter for who he actually was. All I knew was that I would be an adult living any way I chose with the man I loved, the man who had chosen me out of all the beautiful women he could have had. The fact that this belief was a fantasy was soon to become apparent.

Soon after we were married, Peter began to keep me away from my family and indicated he wanted to get away from his as well. To accomplish this he took a job on a dairy farm thirty miles from Alpena. There we moved into a house trailer which had no telephone or even a mailbox to receive letters. The farmer who owned the trailer provided these services and our utilities as part of Peter's pay.

As the Thanksgiving holiday approached, I experienced

the first unusual incident that indicated Peter wanted more than just isolation from outside influences. Thinking to please him, I had planned to prepare Thanksgiving dinner for our families. My grocery list was complete, but, as I headed out the door to purchase the supplies for our feast, Peter stopped me.

"Come back inside," he ordered.

I was taken aback.

Peter explained, "I'm not taking part in any of the traditional holidays with our families. And, since those strange spells of yours keep cropping up, we won't be having friends over either. You might get weird in front of them and embarrass me. You'll stay here alone with me—we'll just have to pray your curse goes away."

"Peter, don't be silly. You're just in a bad mood or something," I said and proceeded once more toward the door.

He grabbed my shoulders, forced me back into the chair, and tore up the grocery list, throwing the pieces at me.

"You want Thanksgiving dinner? You'll have to go out into the field and kill the turkey yourself." He slammed the trailer door so hard that when he left, the curio shelf fell off the wall and crashed to the floor. I was left alone in shock, disbelief and, as his words echoed, anger. He had somehow managed to stir up an emotion within me I had never experienced before—hatred.

As the Christmas season drew closer, Peter reiterated his insistence that there be no formal celebration and we were to stay strictly alone. To insure my compliance with this demand, he made it impossible for me to leave the trailer for any reason. "I'll just keep your car keys," he told me a few days after his initial outburst. He accompanied me each time

I stepped outside for fresh air.

There was no Christmas tree that year, no neatly wrapped gifts nor were there any twinkling colored lights. My family called us on the farmer's phone but Peter quickly cut off their good wishes by pushing down the receiver. He had won, and was going to keep on winning until my will was completely broken. I hated our life but I still believed he loved me. For some reason that I did not fathom, he must have felt this was his way of providing protection. And in one way I could not blame him. My "spells," as he called them, were not only debilitating but produced a series of strange symptoms: skin which burned to a crisp in the sun, watery eyes and headaches. No wonder he didn't want anyone to see me. And as for friends, I'd had none in my life anyway. I scared most people away, sooner or later.

When I became pregnant with my first child that winter, we became even more segregated from the world. I was extremely nauseous and rarely went out. Peter had given our television set away and I was not allowed to read a newspaper or listen to the radio. Near the end of the pregnancy Peter moved us to a town nearly one hundred miles away from Alpena and took a job on another dairy farm. Up to that point, Peter had not even allowed me to see a doctor for the pregnancy. Then he began to worry. He felt whatever my illness was I might have passed it to our child, our "Rosemary's baby" as he cruelly called it. But I told myself that couldn't happen, that there didn't appear to be anything wrong with the baby as it continued to grow and move inside me. It wasn't until Peter informed me the child would be born at home that I seriously questioned the wisdom of the decision I had made in marrying him. I was so terrified! I didn't know anything about giving birth, let alone delivering a baby, and I was sure he didn't either. Despite my fear, I was forced to abide by his wishes. Peter made it clear that it was his final decision and I had to obey him since he was my husband and the head of our home.

Eventually a concerned neighbor stopped by and told Peter, when he mentioned with a laugh that my labor had already lasted three days, that either Peter take me to the hospital or he would himself. For the first time, I saw apprehension and hysteria in Peter's callous face as he drove me to the hospital.

The birth itself was difficult. Lori had an abundance of problems including low birth weight, reduced body temperature and meconium poisoning.

Finally my parents arrived at the hospital.

"We've been separated for so long!" my mother cried through her tears.

My own tears came from deep inside. We held each other, and Mom comforted me just as she had done when I was a child and in pain. It was so healing to be in her arms again. The security of their presence and love made me feel like I was still their little girl.

After three days the doctor allowed me to take the baby home and this time Mom was not going to allow Peter to shut her out. "I'm staying for one month," she announced to Peter. "I'll take care of Lori and Tammy while you're off doing whatever it is you do."

By this time there were no more jobs at the farm and I didn't know where or how Peter came up with the money to pay the rent and buy food.

When Mom's stay ended, I wanted desperately to take

the baby and go with her. Being an adult was not at all what I had anticipated and being Peter's wife on top of that was torturous. Only motherhood itself was a dream come true. I loved Lori so much. She was so beautiful with her long black hair and delicate, angelic features. But my need to care for my infant and myself had to be balanced with my efforts to control Peter's behavior which became increasingly alarming.

Shortly after Mom returned home, Peter began to alter my life even more. One dark night, he approached me as I was feeding Lori and said, "You need to realize that, as my wife, you're obligated to give up your own identity and exist exclusively to serve me."

I followed him silently as he carried a large aluminum trash container into our bedroom and placed it in the middle of the room. Fear mounted inside me once more. It was as if he was demanding some sort of ritual take place to make his statement real and effective. He soon made this evident.

"Now you are to come with me and deposit in this container all of the possessions you have accumulated since you were a child."

I obeyed.

School yearbooks, photo albums, trinkets and momentos of my life—all gone. My personal items of makeup, jewelry, even my razors and pantyhose all were destroyed. The only items I was allowed to keep were my Bible, a hairbrush, a set of underclothes and two maternity dresses I had sewn when I was pregnant with Lori. When it was over and I had thrown away every shred of my prior existence, I watched through the window as Peter dragged the trash can to the backyard and set its contents on fire. For over an hour he stood watching the yellow flames almost as if he was in a trancelike state. The sparks and smoke drifted into the mid-afternoon sky. I felt numb. Fear was now replaced with disbelief and anguish, but in my loneliness I remained as drawn to Peter as he was to the flames.

When there was nothing left but ashes, Peter came back inside the house. Over the next few months, he continued consolidating his power over my life. Likewise, I continued in the existence he had created for me. I tried to obey his every wish, night and day. I dared not say or do anything that would spur more cruel incidents. I tried not to feel anything at all. It was easier than bearing the emotional agony he took so much pleasure in inflicting. And then, when Lori was three months old, I suspected I was pregnant again. It was more than I could bear.

Chapter 3

Trapped

Winter had arrived and there wasn't much food—a little venison, four or five eggs from the chickens left, and some home-canned beets. Peter was gone again. Stomach cramps and vomiting tormented me again during this pregnancy. We had no car so, when there was a little money for food, I had to bundle Lori up, put her in her stroller, and walk two miles into town to buy groceries and then carry them home. On my way into town on a day when I was five months along in the pregnancy, I suddenly felt sharp pains in my lower abdomen. My body crumpled to the ground. The pavement stung my face. No one was in sight, so I had to force myself to crawl to a tree nearby where I could inch myself up and then stumble painfully over to the stroller.

Somehow I managed to walk another mile up the road to a neighbor's house. Fortunately they were home and took us in.

I miscarried within the hour. When it was all over, they tracked Peter down, telling him to take me to the hospital. As soon as we were alone he made it very clear that the entire incident was all my fault and took me home instead.

"Haven't I told you to stay away from the neighbors?" he yelled. "They're liable to see what a freak you are. I ought to teach you what to expect when you disobey me." He raised his hand but did not touch me.

Nevertheless, his anger was terrifying. I was so weak I couldn't even think of taking Lori and getting away. After three days of bleeding and pain, even Peter was convinced that I needed to see a doctor and he took me into town. The miscarriage was confirmed and the doctor also told me I was RH negative and would probably require an injection to prevent abnormalities in any future children I would have. That probability presented itself a month later when I became pregnant for a third time. Peter forbade all types of birth control. Still recovering from the miscarriage and under fire from Peter's incredible mood swings, I wondered if I would even survive another pregnancy.

Things went from bad to worse. We were evicted from our home and when the opportunity to "house sit" for the winter came up, Peter took it. I was not as ill with this pregnancy but the anxiety caused by our financial situation and being thrown out of our place was frightening. Peter allowed me to see a doctor this time, but not on a routine basis. He was angry with me for being too frail to have my babies at home and for being constantly sick. He regularly let me know that, in his view, I was "a freak." Under the pressure from him and the poverty we were forced to live in, I withdrew, only caring for myself and Lori. When he was around we rarely spoke to each other. Periodically, he went off leaving us to fend for ourselves.

It was an exceptionally harsh winter. A blizzard struck every weekend for eight weeks straight. Snow piled up over the windows and an icy wind blew into the house through the gaps between the glass and the frame. I don't know how, but Bob Royce, a state trooper who lived up the road from us, heard that I was pregnant and alone most of the time. He stopped in at least once a week to make sure everything was all right.

Everything was not all right, but I didn't ever let on as to how bad it really was. Each day I wrapped Lori in blankets and laid her on the sofa in front of the fireplace. I wanted her to remain as still as possible so she wouldn't use a lot of energy and become hungry between meals. After we ran out of food, I knew I had to slaughter the chickens myself so we could eat.

That morning I removed Peter's hunting knife from its sheath and trudged out into the field. My desperation continued to increase, never allowing me an opportunity to stop and think about the fact that I had no idea how to kill a chicken. Up ahead, just past a broken-down barbed wire fence, I saw them, five or six birds pecking seed through the snow. Before I knew it, I was running towards them, climbing through the tangled wire and into their midst. Most of the chickens managed to escape as they saw me coming, but there were still a couple that were not so quick. I grabbed the closest one by the throat and tackled the bird. With a swift slice, I slit its neck. This was the first time I had ever killed anything in my life!

I sat beside the dead bird, crying over what I had done. As I looked down at the lifeless body next to me in the snow and saw the blood dripping from my fingers, fury welled up inside me and burst forth in an anguishing sequence of screams. The instrument of death fell out of my trembling hand next to its victim. *Look what I had become.*

I'd never done anything remotely like that before. However, there was no choice. I couldn't allow Lori to starve. Hunger is a cruel instructor.

Like an angel of mercy, Bob, the state trooper, stopped in on the day that we ran out of firewood and were down to our last piece of chicken. The water pipes had frozen. The electricity had been shut off. The few other chickens had all frozen to death and were strewn about the back yard along with our dog who had died from starvation.

When I winced with pain Bob asked, "Are you ill?"

I explained, "I've been having bad cramps on and off for the past week and my husband's away again."

The trooper stared at me. "Do you have a phone?"

"I'm afraid not."

"I'll be right back. I'm going to find you some place warm to stay." He went out to his car and called from his radio. Within half an hour a minister and his wife, Reverend and Mrs. Tupper, arrived. They kindly gathered Lori and me up and took us to their home.

Lori was so cold and malnourished that I did not even consider my own predicament. Her hands and feet were blue and she had obviously lost weight. It took several days of feeding Lori small quantities of food before she was able to eat anything without it coming right back up. Mrs. Tupper strongly urged that I go back to the doctor. "I'll take you even if it means going behind your husband's back," she said. She was such a kind caring lady, I could tell she was incensed that I had been abused. I had been spotting and was also not able to keep any of the food down that she prepared for me. The baby seemed enormous inside of me. Just walking across the room took enormous effort.

Reverend Tupper told my husband that I needed medical attention and needed it promptly. His wife phoned the doctor's office, but he was out of town until the next day. After she explained the predicament to the nurse, it was decided to take me directly to the hospital and word would be left for the doctor to go there upon his return.

I could see the anger and humiliation in his eyes when Peter arrived at the hospital, but I knew he would not dare act on it in front of other people. It was the only comfort I had at that point.

The nurse came to give me a routine examination. As she placed the stethoscope on my oddly rounded belly, she jumped back in astonishment.

Fearing the worst—perhaps my baby had no heart-beat—I mustered the courage to ask what was wrong.

"Well, my dear. Either your baby is having a heart attack or there are two of them in there!"

My shock at her statement made me speechless. My mind spun. Two! I had been worried that I couldn't even care for one properly no less two more.

X-rays were taken immediately and, sure enough, there were two babies, about five pounds each. The nurse placed an emergency call to the doctor with the new information. "She's now dilated to five but no active labor. Yes...Yes."

She hung up and walked over to us. "The doctor said he will be arriving by nightfall and he'll most likely induce labor at that time."

My body and mind were so exhausted I couldn't think.

Peter was ecstatic at the news of twins and uncharacteristi-
cally began calling his family. It didn't matter to me what he
did or thought at that point as long as he called my mother.
Amazingly, he did. I tried to sleep. If I slept, there was the
possibility that I would wake to find this was all a nightmare.
In a short while I would be the mother of three children. We
had no home, no money, no jobs. The future in front of me
appeared as a big, black, gaping hole. What were we going to
do? How would we go on? I wrestled with these questions,
finding no peace or answers.

Later that evening the doctor arrived as promised and
induced labor. Three hours later I gave birth to the first baby,
my son, Danny. He came into the world quickly and quietly.
With a deep breath, a yawn and a lusty cry Danny rolled back
over and continued his slumber. The other baby still inside me
was being considerably more obstinate. After an hour without
further labor I was beginning to think the twin theory was just
a big joke! The doctor assured me this was no joke and he
would have to put me to sleep because the baby's head was
caught under my ribcage. He had a sense of urgency in his
voice. The baby's heart rate was strong and constant, but mine
had soared to 200 beats per minute. The nurses began moving
hastily around me. The next thing I knew they placed a mask
over my face and the sound of loud bells rang in my ears.
Then darkness.

A minute, an hour, an eternity passed. Suddenly, the
screaming of a newborn baby shook the air. I sat up with a
jolt that shocked everyone in the delivery room. The doctor
was holding up my tiny daughter up so I could see her. She
was beautiful! This exquisite newborn creature was looking
directly into my eyes, shrieking and spitting and shaking as

though she was furious with me for having been put through such a trauma. I was instantly drawn to her hands. They were absolutely perfect, ivory in color with the longest, most dainty fingers. The doctor handed my new daughter to the nurse to be cleaned and weighed.

Then the nurses brought the babies to me and I held them close, feeling apprehension for the future. The doctor leaned over us and spoke softly. He said he had some trouble delivering the second baby, but everything turned out just fine. "They weigh six and one-half pounds each and are healthy. Congratulations. You did a fine job." Seeing my beautiful newborns, I felt a momentary surge of hope. The future was unknown to me, but these two new lives were two miracles that could not be ignored. I felt honored to have had the experience of birth.

Peter named our new daughter Johanna after his mother. "It's the right thing to do and it's a good strong name for such a strong young lady." I felt that if he named the baby it could signify a new beginning for all of us. Perhaps Johanna's and Dan's births would wake him up to his responsibilities.

They didn't.

Shortly after I was settled back in my hospital room, Peter left. He never came to take us home, wherever that might be. Mom and Dad waited with me for four days and then made the decision to take us all home with them. In many ways it was a relief! I knew we would all be loved and cared for there. Still, my heart was breaking. After three weeks at my parents' home, Peter finally called. "I've spent all this time looking for a job and have found one down by Jackson, where my parents live. We'll have to live with them for a while."

The entire time he was gone I had felt utterly abandoned. Why didn't he at least call and let me know where he
was? He could have been dead all that time and I wouldn't
even have known! Mom tried hard to convince me to stay
with them and not go back. "I've bought everything you need
to take care of these two new babies and bought Lori some
decent clothes as well. Stay here with us where all of you will
be safe." It was an offer I considered seriously, but despite her
generosity, mother worked and had awful episodes of illness.
It would be for the best to have my family back together.
Perhaps Peter would finally see his mistakes and the pain he
had caused. If this was true, I had to try to be forgiving. So, I
went back to him.

Chapter 4

Another Glimpse of Darkness

We lived with my in-laws for several months. Peter did have a job and went to work faithfully every day. But I was told not to ask for his mother's help. She had just given birth to another child. Between cooking, cleaning and trying to care for my own babies, I had little time to spare. Breast-feeding took two hours each feeding so, by the time I was done with one baby, the other was ready to eat again. And I had to keep the house spotless or Peter would rant for hours. The physical and emotional stress was too much—I had an attack of the strange illness which still plagued me. I asked my mother if it could be the same sickness which beset her. "No...impossible," she said and changed the subject. I had become so accustomed to the presence of endless illness that I did not question her abrupt response. Still I felt even then that she was holding something back. However, it was her stoic example that kept me going. If she could bear being so ill in silence, so could I.

I became a withered, hollow shell of myself with

absolutely no energy. Stomach cramps and headaches plagued me. Open sores blistered my back and arms. Peter said nothing. Not *What's wrong?* or *Should we call a doctor?* Of course, he believed I was cursed and had no use for doctors. The only thing he told me was not to go anywhere or invite anyone over. I knew he was ashamed of me, but I could do nothing to stop what my body was doing to me. Finally, Peter moved us into a house trailer far from his parents and even farther from mine.

Not long afterward, Peter quit his job and began drinking and taking drugs. Although he'd been verbally and emotionally abusive to me for some time, now he also took his anger out on the children. Then he just gave up altogether and left for weeks at a time. One night, just as I had prepared supper, without a word to any of us, he reappeared, picked up his plate of food, shoved it in my face and smeared it across my clothes. With a sinister laugh he sneered, "Now all of you looks as disgusting as your face and body does. You freak!"

This time when he left, a month went by. The electricity was once again shut off. The gas tanks ran dry, leaving us without heat. And on top of everything I was pregnant again. I felt trapped in his vicious routine of torture.

Somehow the children and I existed. However, I became extremely ill in my seventh month of the pregnancy. This time it was Peter's family that convinced him I needed to see a doctor. The doctor thought I had gestational diabetes and edema. The baby was growing at an alarming rate! At thirty-two weeks gestation the child was already thought to weigh over nine pounds. My heart raced constantly and a murmur was suspected, making the situation even more dangerous.

Despite the fact that my mother was having a serious attack I called upon my parents once more for help. I began to realize there was no hope for my marriage. I wanted to divorce Peter. Anything was better than the way the children and I were being forced to exist, but somehow I couldn't seem to act on that realization. Do I really have any hope of a better future? I asked myself despairingly.

Mom came right away despite her attack and the professional burden that tax season placed on her at the accounting firm. Immediately upon her arrival she had all of the utilities reinstalled and the gas tanks filled. "Tammy, Dad and I can't stand to see you, Lori and the twins live like this. We tried to give you everything and now you're living worse than a trailer person. We wanted better for you than we have, not worse. I'm an accountant. You never even went to college. And Peter doesn't even work steadily. Please come home with us. We'll take care of the kids. We'll send you back to school."

"I just can't," I said. "I have to try and make this marriage work. Mom, no one else ever looked at me or wanted me."

"Tammy," my mother said sadly, "Peter calls you names because you're ill and attacks you while you're pregnant. Do you think that's love?"

When Peter returned he treated Mom as an intruder and me as a traitor. He was no longer concerned with hiding his abuse of me. My mother bought the food, cooked the meals, cleaned the house and looked after the children. Peter felt this was my responsibility whether I was ill or not. Night after night he deliberately started arguments with her. When she refused to back down, he left shouting obscenities to both of us. Days later he returned and started to argue with her all over again.

We lived in this atmosphere of armed warfare for weeks until it was time for me to give birth, but the baby took his time coming into the world. Perhaps he could sense the chaos he was about to become a part of. According to the doctor's calculations, he was five weeks overdue. Every other day Mom would take me to the hospital for tests to ensure the baby's safety and to monitor his growth. Finally, Mom had been there well over a month and had to get back to her business before there was no business. "I hate leaving you, Tammy, but if I lose my job I won't be able to help either of us."

Labor began the day after she left. It was long and difficult. The baby was not breathing when he was born. The doctor massaged his back and rubbed the bottom of his feet until Reuben took his first breath. After his birth I was exhausted which was to be expected, but there were other strange problems. My stomach cramps continued as did the accelerated heart rate. The doctor kept me in the hospital for eight days and, despite the pain, I slept nearly the entire time. Again there was no diagnosis of why I had such severe complications. They finally abated and I was able to go home.

Our dysfunctional family life continued to deteriorate after Reuben was born. Naturally, all my time was taken up with the care of the children.

One of Peter's favorite methods of torture was to lock me in our bedroom and listen outside the door to me beg and plead for him to let me out. He had nailed all the windows shut so even had I wanted to escape, there was no way without breaking the glass. Peter knew I wouldn't even attempt this. I would never leave him without taking the children with me. He seemed to receive particular pleasure from gathering the children outside the door and telling my babies that I needed to stay locked in because I was turning into a *scary monster* and would hurt them. Peter had finally found a way to cause the most excruciating pain of all; he used my appearance to terrify the children. Each time this happened I seemed to have another attack which brought on more and more physical symptoms which disabled my body. His mental torture had the same effect on my mind. By this time, despite my efforts to cling to the only relationship I'd ever had and to my children's father I knew he didn't love me. He never had and never would. Marriage, I was raised to believe, is a sacred institution and if there is even the slightest shred of hope in salvaging the union, I would have to continue to try. One day, however, I overheard Peter talking to one of his friends. He was telling him that he was fed up with me claiming to be sick all the time. The children and I were a burden, hindering him from living as he should. He wished we were dead.

A few days later I was occupied with my chores, drying the last of the silverware and wiping down the counter when, out of the corner of my eye, I caught a glimpse of Reuben crawling into his father's lap. Somehow, our ten-month-old son had managed to climb out of his crib and down the stairs, which surprised both of us. As I casually reached for the baby to put him back in bed, I couldn't help thinking how grown up he was becoming. His inquisitive nature had developed suddenly as well and was leading him to new and wondrous discoveries. Peter, on the other hand, did not find his son's actions something at which to marvel. He flew into a tremendous

rage, screaming at the baby and then pushing me into the
bookcase. When I reached for Reuben, Peter's violent outburst caught me off guard, finally transforming me into the
scared, shaking animal he had labored so long to create. The
maternal instinct to protect my child was stronger than my
fear. It was the jolt back into reality that I had needed for so
long. The power of my mother's instinct forced me to struggle back to my feet. Peter proceeded to drag Reuben by his
arm up the stairs and into the bedroom. Running after him, I
arrived at the bedroom door and watched helplessly as Peter
pounded furiously on the baby's bare bottom. Reuben
shrieked in terror and pain at each stinging blow. "Stop," I
screamed, but it was as if I wasn't even there. When Peter
was finished, he threw our nearly lifeless child back into the
crib and pushed me out of his way as he stumbled back
downstairs to his chair.

The rest of the night, I held my hurting infant in my
arms. He clung tightly to my body as we rocked back and
forth on the bedroom floor, crying ourselves to sleep. In the
morning, as I surveyed the blood-crusted cuts amongst the
black and blue bruises on my child's body, I knew we had to
get away. For days I made secret plans.

Because Peter knew of my fear of driving in snowy
conditions, I decided that the children and I should leave
when a storm had been forecast. The night we all left, the
Tuppers arranged a police escort to the county line, giving us
thirty miles of protection. In a raging blizzard, I drove the
children to my parents' home. It took seven hours to drive
ninety miles—and we never looked back!

Dad set me up in a small house and Mom set me up
with a tubal ligation. I agreed to the operation. Even though

I loved my children, I could not imagine ever wanting more. The doctor thought that because I was only twenty-two years old and had many more childbearing years ahead I could eventually change my mind. However, after much discussion, he reluctantly consented to perform the operation. I knew I had no choice.

Winter was cold and storm-filled, but this time we were safe and warm in our new home and life. My brother, Dan, stayed with us quite often, both to help out with the children and to keep an eye out for Peter, who had been making threatening phone calls to me. Everything went wonderfully until early spring when my soon-to-be ex-husband decided to break into the house. Dan phoned my father and the sheriff as Peter held two of the children in his arms. He blurted out massive amounts of foul language and threatened to take the children away from me. My dad subdued him. Afterwards, my parents helped me get a lawyer to handle the divorce.

Chapter 5

A Semblance of Peace

When my divorce from Peter became final, my parents convinced me to go back to college full-time and to work part-time. They would give me and the children some extra help. That way I would become self-sufficient sooner. Between school, work and homework I had to savor every opportunity to be with my children.

One summer day, a few months later, I woke up with horrible shooting pains in my back. The doctor whom I visited said it was a torn muscle. Although I had never experienced a torn muscle, it didn't seem to me like that was the problem. I hadn't been doing anything strenuous involving my back to cause such ferocious pain. Then other symptoms began. My skin broke out in red splotches. The doctor suggested that the stress I had been under from school and work was most likely the cause of the stomach pains. I had to wear sunglasses because when I went outside my eyes teared, blurring my vision. People stared at me wherever I went. Once again, after several weeks, I recovered.

I had no time to think about my health or appearance. I redoubled my efforts to become self-supporting. I worked all day and even took a full load of classes during the summer session in order to obtain my degree in criminal justice that much sooner. Fortunately, I was able to find two retired women, excellent baby-sitters, who looked after the children and charged very little. With plenty of food, a warm supportive environment, and the loving attention of my family, their health soon returned. Even though I was not able to be home as a full-time mother, we all felt safe and content. For the first time, we had hope.

My last year in college brought many changes but one recurrent problem. I was still having strange attacks of illness and the attitudes of others who saw me during them remained, as they had all my life, cruel and unfeeling.

"Tammy, could I see you in my office for a moment after class?" Professor Hagan waited for my response from across the crowded classroom.

For the entire hour I had been desperately trying not to draw any kind of attention to myself. The sores were back again, the embarrassing blisterlike boils that appeared on my skin out of nowhere and without warning. I cupped my hand around my face, burying my head in the textbook. It was a feeble attempt to remain inconspicuous, like just another face in the crowd. The more I tried to hide myself from my class-mates, the more intently they stared at me.

Usually I came to class early, long before the other students arrived in order to take a seat in the far corner of the room. On this Tuesday I hadn't planned on coming at all, but because I had missed so much work that semester I couldn't afford not to. I knew that people always became insatiably curious about something they think they are not supposed to see.

"Yes, Mr. Hagan," I said, managing to squeak a response from behind my paperback barricade.

I waited in my seat until the other students, down to the last one, left the room. Each one passed my desk in slow motion it seemed. Their eyes, I felt, pierced through the pages of my book like finely honed daggers, hoping to get a closer look. I tried to tell myself I was just being paranoid. However, as I gazed slightly above the binding, I realized that it was not just a delusion. They *were* staring! Most of the others in the law enforcement program were men, young and strong, with athletic physiques. In contrast to the attention they paid to the other women in class, they had been repelled by my presence from the beginning, noting my often scab-covered face and shapeless clothes. Once again I was an intruder, a crack in the glass orb of passing beauty. And now, in the midst of my worse attack, they perceived me as a freak.

I hoped the professor would show more compassion as I entered his office. His back was turned to me as he riffled through a pile of papers at his file cabinet. A wisp of cherry-scented pipe smoke rose in a feathery stream over the shoulder of his gray wool jacket. "Mr. Hagan, it's Tammy," I said shyly.

"Come on in and have a seat, Tammy. I have a couple of things I need to discuss with you." As he turned to greet me, his eyes grazed my face with a twinge of embarrassment. My heart pounded violently from the uncomfortable tension in the room.

"Let's sit down," he said. "You've been cowering in the back of the classroom all morning. Are you having some kind of adolescent breakout or haven't you been getting enough? What's the matter with your face?" He looked down. "I can only imagine what you're hiding under that turtleneck sweater."

I reddened. Tears rose in my eyes. I sat down slowly in the chair, astonished at what I was hearing. His cruel remarks humiliated and amazed me!

For the past three and a half years this man had been my professor, my mentor for a career in criminal justice. I had worked hard to prove myself to him, certainly much harder than anyone else had to. Up until now, Mr. Hagan had always been polite, but distant with me. The entire time I had been under his guidance he never tolerated any open displays of disrespect towards me, by my classmates. I thought it was because he was one of those rare compassionate human beings who didn't judge people on appearance. Now he had acted worse than they. The most disgusting part of it was that he presumed to be familiar with the details that caused my unsightly condition. Obviously, even though I had been absent from class on many occasions, it never entered his mind that I might be ill. Despite my annoyance over his remarks, I knew I had to be careful how I responded to them. My future was in his hands. My chance for a career to support my family depended on his assessment of me. He could bring that possibility crashing down around me with a stroke of his pen.

"You said you had something important to discuss with me?" I reminded him, trying to regain my composure.

"Oh? Oh yes, that's right," he said. "I wanted to give you this."

"What is it?" I asked, holding the papers he had handed me.

"That, my dear, is an employment application for the correctional facility in Ypsilanti. Actually, it's more of a survey of sorts, to see if you would even qualify for the application process. Each fall they send me two applications and ask me to give them to the students I feel would be most suited to the job. Do you think it might be something you'd be interested in?"

"I'm afraid I don't know what to say. I never expected anything like this!"

"Well, I've given it a lot of thought. Till today I thought you might be well qualified, but now. . . ."

Oh God, I thought, *please don't let him hold my hideous blisters against me. Please let him see it's not my fault.*

He went on. "Well, it's their call anyway. If you're eventually chosen for this program, there would be a lengthy training session and possibly even a transfer to another part of the country. Would that be a problem?" He stared at me, seeming to scan each inch of my face.

"I don't think so, but I really don't know," I replied. "I really need a job badly. I have four children, you know."

He looked surprised at this revelation also. I sighed heavily.

I was holding in my hand the golden opportunity of a lifetime. All the long hours of strenuous physical training and grueling late night study sessions had been worth this one special moment. It was like a dream come true! The odds for my attaining a promising position had been against me from the beginning. Most of the prestigious jobs would be given to the men in the program who displayed above average ability. The rest of us, especially the few women, would probably be placed as security guards or dispatchers in small town police stations. Despite that, I had worked hard, doing every extra credit assignment possible as well as turning in massive papers to overcome such obstacles to attain the rank of "the chosen."

"Well, take the application home and think about the offer. There's still a couple of weeks before it has to be returned."

"Thank you, Mr. Hagan."

"Hey, just doin' my job." He smiled.

"Was there anything else you needed to speak to me about?" I asked, rising.

"No, I guess that's about it. I'll see you in the morning," he said, scanning my face again and wincing as he relit his pipe.

"Yes, sir, bright and early as always," I confirmed as I headed toward the door, nearly forgetting my uneasiness over his previous comments.

"Oh, Tammy." He fondled his chin once more. "You should probably put something on that. Looks like it really hurts." He smirked again.

I walked away from him, responding to his ignorance in my head. *Yes, Mr. Hagan, it hurts, but not in the way you think! My pain is deeper than you are capable of realizing!* Tears of humiliation ran down my face as I made my way through the crowded hallway, its walls lined with rows of faceless, gaping strangers. They turned their backs to me in disgust as I passed by them, whispering to each other. *I know what you're saying about me,* I thought desperately, willing myself to hold back my tears until I could once again be alone. *I know what you're saying about me. Do you think I am not aware of what I look like? This is not the first time my face has been deformed by an attack. You've just never seen*

*me look as bad as this before . . . and you are afraid of me
because I am different.*
I ran with my head down. The application for the correctional facility job stared up into my swollen, blistered
face. The clean white pages crumpled between my fingers,
wadding up into a ball in the palm of my hand. *I knew I
would never send it in. I'm going home to hide from you. In
time you will forget what you have seen when you looked at
me like this. You have that luxury. My only consolation is in
the knowledge that you are a bunch of ignorant fools. I may
eventually return to normal. But that may not happen for
weeks or as much as a month. For all of you it may be never.
All of you are prisoners of your fear. You have made me a
captive of your injustice. How many times have I wished to
possess the key to the confinement I endure, the confinement
based on your ignorance. Too many to count, it seems. For
now all I can do is run from you and hide.*

Chapter 6

Thoughts and Fears

Over the next few days I could not stop thinking about what had happened. Loneliness had followed me most of my life. It was not a stranger, not a friend. It was just there. Sometimes I longed for companionship. Not that the children and my family didn't hold a large part of my heart, but I was still young and wanted to love and be loved. I wanted to find someone to share my thoughts, someone whom I could support and cherish, and who would, for the first time, offer to love and listen to me.

Of course, I knew that my chances for meeting that special someone were slim.

Whatever my illness was, it estranged me from others, especially men. Look at how Peter had treated me. Look at Mr. Hagan. I told myself to accept my state, cherish my children, and realize that it would be hard for any man, even if my appearance didn't put him off, to become a stepfather to four children not his own.

However, at the end of the term, one of the students,

Jill, decided to hold a class party. To my surprise, she invited me. I wasn't going to attend, thinking my presence would only mar the festivities, but the children and my parents urged me to go, knowing I had almost no social life. Mother took me to buy a new party dress, my first in years. It was simple and sensuous, made of navy blue silk. Trying it on in front of their admiring eyes, I prayed I wouldn't have another breakout.

I didn't. The night of the party soon came. Looking in the mirror just before I left the house, seeing my long brown hair softly styled, the dress clinging to the curves of my body, I actually felt pretty.

Walking into the room filled with students, I could see from their astonished eyes that they too saw the difference. Even so, few talked to me. The easy, relaxed camaraderie they had with each other tensed whenever I joined a group. And then Jill brought over a friend of hers, Tim Evans, and I was glad I came.

He was tall, very tall, like my stepfather. I had to bend my head all the way back just to look into his eyes. Although most women would find this uncomfortable, I didn't. Tim's warm dark eyes had a soothing effect on my spirit. His neatly dressed physique, clean-shaven face and polite handshake attracted me. As the night progressed, he stayed at my side. I felt I wanted to find out more about him and to my surprise he seemed to feel the same. We ended up talking for hours and found that we had many similar experiences. We both carried scars; his from exposing his heart to the wrong person and I from Peter and the isolation of my disease. A bond was created between us. I told Tim about the ordeal which I'd been through physically and personally and a little about my marriage. I knew even at this first meeting that if he was going to retreat from me it had to be quickly before I fell hopelessly in love.

He didn't run away. In fact, over the next few weeks as we got to know each other, he began to encourage me on a daily basis. He told me he found my blossoming strength and independence to be attractive qualities.

Our first kiss was magical! It wasn't spontaneous, but planned and choreographed. Tim made me feel like I wanted to be kissed, and asked permission to do so. The respect he had for me as a woman as well as a person was evident in his every word and action. Real love was a new and exhilarating experience. I felt a sense of security whenever we were together.

His caring, sheltering manner formed a protective shield that I had never experienced before, except from my parents. His gentleness and quiet strength attracted me even more. However, I still carried with me fear induced by the cruelty of my first husband and the ignorant people I'd met in my school and community. I was extremely cautious. Tim was patient and understanding. It was obvious from the beginning that Tim adored my children and enjoyed their company. Soon they felt the same way. Eventually, we all felt secure in his care. Tim even took a job in Alpena so I wouldn't have to leave my parents. We were married the following summer under the pink blossoms of a cherry tree in my parents' back yard. The decision to become his wife was the best I'd ever made.

During our courtship, Tim had never seen me experience one of my strange attacks. Then, about two months later, I had a break-out at the corner of my mouth. Tender pink bumps appeared and formed a rash that spread down my chin and to my back. Within days the angry sores burst open, burning and itching with vengeful intensity. I was so afraid he wouldn't love me any more when he saw them. That night, as I was getting ready for bed, Tim called to me.

"Come sit beside me for a minute, hon," he said, with a look of concern and compassion.

I sat down next to him on the bed, afraid of what he might say. He scanned my face and then gently brushed back the satin fabric of my robe exposing the broken skin.

"It happens sometimes," I tried to explain. "I don't know why, but it does."

Tim caressed my arms with his loving touch. "It just looks so painful."

"It is."

He focused his attention on my left shoulder, lightly touching the skin around one of the boils. "Don't you have a birthmark on this side of your back?"

I giggled a little. "Well, of course I do, silly. You know that! It's so big, how could you miss it!"

Tim wasn't laughing. Instead, a tone of fear entered his voice. "Honey, it's not there anymore. There's nothing but a huge red bump the size of a quarter, with a lot of little white ones all around it."

That birthmark had always been there. I had often wished it would fade away over time, but not like this. I walked over to the vanity mirror, trying to see what he had described. "I had no idea."

"I want you to make an appointment tomorrow morning to have that looked at. You can't fool around with things like this, Tam. It could be serious."

I didn't sleep well that night. Horror stories of skin

cancer raced through my mind. I wondered if it might be too late for me.

After doing my best to describe my condition to my local doctor's nurse, she set me up with one of our local surgeons that same afternoon. Dr. Benton didn't say anything about the rash itself. He focused only on the spot that Tim had noticed the night before, where the birthmark used to be.

"You say its been there all your life?" he asked, touching it gingerly.

"Well, yes. It's a birthmark. I was born with it."

"It wasn't a mole, with raised edges?"

I was feeling increasingly uncomfortable with the way in which he was referring to it in the past tense. "No. I told you. It's just a patch of dark skin."

He carefully prodded at it some more, mumbling to himself as he did. Finally, he came around and stood in front of me. "I would suggest that we remove it immediately and have it tested. I can do it right here in the office."

Panic came over me at once, pounding with each rush of blood through my veins. I remembered all too well the last time I had surgery and the months of illness and recuperation from it. His suggestion terrified me, I wanted to leave.

"Isn't there another way to test it?" I begged him. "Can't you just put some ointment on it or something and see if that makes it go away?"

"Listen, Tammy. We're talking about a possible malignant melanoma here. That isn't anything to fool around with. The sooner it's removed, the better we'll both feel about it."

Reluctantly, I submitted. As the nurse prepared his

tray of instruments, he tried to calm my nervousness. "After the initial injection of anesthetic, you won't feel anything. It will be over within less than ten minutes," he reassured me. "Just one thing, though. I don't want you to drive home by yourself. Is there someone you would like the nurse to call, someone to pick you up?"

I gave her Tim's work number and asked her to explain to him that it was not an emergency. I didn't want him to break any traffic laws getting there.

My body was trembling as the doctor placed the blue paper sheet over my back. The injection stung a little, but within less than a minute I felt nothing but an odd sensation of pressure. "That was the most painful part, Tammy. In just a few minutes, it will be all over and you'll be ready to go home."

I could hear the sound of the scalpel piercing my skin and sliding along my back. Then I felt a tug each time Dr. Benton tied a stitch. "There will be four stitches on the inside and eight on the outside. I'm going to want to see you again in seven days, so I can remove them and see how you're doing."

"What about the testing? How long will it take to find out the results?" I asked.

"I'll have the sample sent up to the lab this afternoon. I should know something within a day or two. I'll call you as soon as I get them back."

My panic attack had subsided, thanks to the doctor's gentle manner. After he was finished sewing me up, I even had the nerve to look at what he had removed. Floating in a clear liquid solution was a large chunk of reddish-blue skin. It looked like a slice of blueberry pie rather than a clump of human tissue. He had dug down close to an inch under the wound. It felt kind of funny seeing a part of my body floating in a jar like that. But he was right. I did feel a sense of relief that, whatever it was, it was gone.

Dr. Benton gave me a prescription for antibiotics and told me to take them until he saw me again. "Now, after that stuff wears off, you're going to be in some pain. Here." He whipped off another sheet from his prescription pad. "I want you to take this pain medication as directed on the bottle."

"Thank you for being so kind, Dr. Benton. I acted like a big baby and it was nice of you to be so understanding."

"Not at all. It is scary to have this kind of procedure done. Tammy, I want you to rest at home for a few days. Just take it easy. You look as though you could use it."

Tim was pacing back and forth, waiting anxiously for me in the reception area, when I came out. Even though the nurse had told him it wasn't urgent, he'd raced right over. "Is everything all right?"

"Yes, hon. I'm fine. The doctor had to remove the birth-mark to have it tested. He'll call in a couple of days with the results." I was acting all tough and brave, now that it was over.

Tim took me home and tucked me into bed before going to fill the prescriptions. Over the next couple of days, I grew weaker. Within minutes after taking the medication each time, nausea engulfed me and I felt dizzy. Tim sat with me, day and night through the weekend, doing what he could to make me more comfortable. Monday morning, Dr. Benton called with the results.

"As you probably suspected, there were some indications of skin cancer. However, there wasn't anything detected in the surrounding tissues or in the blood stream, and that's good."

I was relieved at his diagnosis, but my current ailments were what were really beginning to frighten me. "Dr. Benton, ever since I started taking the antibiotics and pain medicine, I've been so sick to my stomach. I think I'm going to stop taking them. That won't hurt anything, will it?"

"You can stop the pain medication. It's been a few days and I think you can handle any pain on your own. But I would advise against stopping the antibiotic. You had a lot of unusual infection at the site, Tammy, and I'd like to have that all cleared up as soon as possible. How is your rash doing?"

I thought he hadn't even noticed it when I was in his office. It would have been kind of hard for him not to. "It's much better, actually. It started to clear up the day after the surgery."

"I thought it probably would. From what you've told me about yourself, I suspected that it was mostly psychosomatic."

"Are you telling me that it was all in my head?" I was perturbed that he would say such a thing.

"No, Tammy," he laughed. "That's not what I'm saying at all. You have been spreading yourself pretty thin the past few months. What I'm trying to tell you is that stress has a funny way of creeping up on a person. When it gets to be too much to handle, it can present its effects in all kinds of different ways, like the rash. I think you just need to rest for a few days and then take it slow from there."

I stopped taking all of the medication, even though Dr. Benton said that I shouldn't. I was sure that it was what had been making me sick. As soon as I was off it, the nausea and dizziness melted away. Within a week, when I saw the doctor the next time, the rash, and all of the other symptoms were completely gone. Tim and I went on with our new life together, never giving the episode a second thought.

Tim petitioned the court to adopt my four children. This didn't seem like it was going to be a problem, as my ex-husband hadn't even visited them in a long time and had never paid child support either. However, just days before the judge was prepared to grant the adoption, my ex-husband contested it and put us through major battles in the legal system. He never gave us or the judge a reason why. He *didn't* want them—I knew that. He just saw this as an opportunity to torture me one more time. Each time I had to face him in the courtroom it brought back all the terror the children and I had lived through. Tim was strong for me and never gave up the fight. He had earned the right to be recognized as the children's father. Ultimately, the judge ruled in our favor. We legally became "the Evans family."

We felt life had finally begun to be all we'd dreamed about.

Nevertheless, it wasn't long after that when I became ill again with yet another ailment that seemed to baffle medical science. Some of the symptoms, such as the stomach cramps, were the same. Only this time the intensity was much more severe. The pain in my back that had been treated previously as a torn muscle was more pervading. And a new symptom appeared on my body in the form of a rash that spread tiny red bumps all over my torso. After seeing two different doctors, a gynecologist and an internal medicine practitioner, I received the diagnoses that there were two separate ailments. I was diagnosed as having ovarian cysts, which would explain the cramps and back pain. For this, one doctor prescribed a mild birth control pill which he felt would dissolve the cysts. The tiny red bumps on my face and body were diagnosed as German measles. The internist believed that even though I had been inoculated against the disease as a child, it must have been a faulty dose. For this he said I needed to take tetracycline, an antibiotic. Even though both diagnosises seemed odd to Tim and me, we accepted the wisdom of the doctors and I began the treatments for the ailments.

After a week or so on both medications, I became violently ill. The birth control pill caused me to bleed profusely. I was unable to even get out of bed without the blood gushing onto the floor. The tetracycline affected my equilibrium so badly that as soon as I lifted my head off the pillow the room began spinning. I had severe nausea. This went on for days before Tim and I decided together that I would stop both medications and see if that helped. It did!

Each day I grew stronger and within a couple of weeks I was able to return to my last semester at college. Although I was weak, I needed to press on to catch up on what I had missed in order to graduate, which I did that May.

The children, my parents, Tim and I had a wonderful celebration.

Things were definitely looking up.

Chapter 7

Legacies

Unfortunately, early that August we received news from my natural father that he had moved his parents from their apartment in Sault Ste. Marie in the Upper Peninsula to a nursing home in Gaylord, just an hour's drive from Alpena. Even after my parents divorced, I enjoyed a warm and loving relationship with my father's parents. I still remembered the day when grandma had come to our house to help me understand my mother's illness, "poor fear." As I grew I spent many vacations at their cottage on the St. Mary's River. We spent time together on a regular basis. Grandma had treated me with great favoritism. At times I could sense this was a source of antagonism to some of my aunts and uncles, but Grandma didn't seem to care. She never explained to me or anyone else why I was her favorite and, as the matriarch of our family, she didn't have to. As far as any of us knew, I hadn't ever done anything in particular to attain this rank of favor in my grandmother's eyes. I had simply been born. For her, that was enough.

When Tim and I had taken the children to see them earlier that year the grandparents had not mentioned that there was even the likelihood that they would have to be moved to a home. Grandma baked an apple cake and prepared her famous roast beef dinner. The children and I pored through countless albums of family photos which had become a tradition whenever going to visit my grandparents. Tim and Grandpa sneaked off to the garage, chatting endlessly over beers about fishing, hunting, and "the way things were back in my day." Grandpa adored Tim, and I think he even saw a little of himself in my husband.

There was no reason to suspect that these two wonderful people were incapable of living on their own. Perhaps they didn't want to worry Tim and me with the news of my biological father's decision to put them in a nursing home. More likely, I suspect they themselves were not even aware of the plans others had made for their lives. The entire situation shocked and bewildered us. Other than their age, there didn't seem to be a reason for them to be there. Neither of my grandparents had any family or ties in Gaylord. I failed to understand why they were being sent to a place far from all of us. The only reason that was explained to me was that it was the only home available in Michigan.

I found this particularly difficult to believe. On several occasions I pleaded with my father to let them live with us, but he said no, reminding me that it was his decision. I made weekly visits and, when Tim's schedule permitted it, he would join me. It was so sad to see them in the horrible place, knowing I did not have the power to change their circumstance. It would break my heart to listen to them weep like little children, begging me to take them with me each time I would leave. Their will to live drained away quickly in that sterile, inattentive environment. My grandmother soon became desperately ill. I was with her constantly the week before she died. Never having witnessed death, I didn't realize that it could be such an emotionally exhausting experience. She had always been a vibrant woman, full of life and enthusiasm. Perhaps she clung to life with every ounce of energy she possessed because of this vitality. The part of my life that had come from her love and companionship was dying with her and the pain was overwhelming.

One day toward the end, I held Grandma's hand for hours, while Grandpa sat stoically in the corner of the room. *It's not supposed to be this way,* I agonized to myself. Each day, for the three days, I had come here and smelled the putrid odor of cheap disinfectant suffocating and strong in the cramped hospital room. Out of the window I could see a gust of early winter wind ruffling the boughs of the pine trees. How I longed to breathe in its sweet cleansing aroma and feel the crispness of its sting against my skin! The constant beep of her heart monitor regulated the hours that passed ever so slowly. From beyond the door to the room there was the occasional squeak of a nurse's shoes scurrying along on the freshly waxed tile floor. I stared at her hand as I held it. It was withered and cold. Purplish, vein-wrapped bones protruded through the transparent film of her skin. It was unrecognizable to me. Could this be the same hand that rubbed my stomach when it hurt, or pet my forehead when I had a fever? The function of nurturer had been reversed. It was my turn to care for her, as she had done for me. She was dying. I had resigned myself to that. Her time had come, and there was nothing I could do to stop the inevitable.

We were alone, Grandma, Grandpa and me, in this sterile unfamiliar environment. Where had everyone gone? All the people she had given so much of herself to throughout her life, her sons and their families, her friends, were not by her side. Cookouts and parties at the cottage, songs sung gleefully around the piano, roast beef dinners with apple cake for dessert—all gone. Our years together played back in my head in jumbled frames.

"Keep these memories close to your heart," she whispered to me. "They are our valuable treasures and now I leave them to you."

Those were her last words before she closed her eyes in eternal sleep.

I watched her sleep. It was quiet now. Too quiet. We were alone together. And soon, I would be without her.

"How ya holdin' up, kiddo." The nonchalant voice of my father awakened me from my trancelike state. He nodded curtly at his father. His hand squeezed my shoulder in an attempt to provide comfort. It was too late for comfort or consoling! He should have been here days ago! He should have gotten in his car and driven here immediately when I called him! Instead, he left Grandpa and me here to face her death alone.

"Where have you been?" I snapped at him. "I called you three days ago and you said you were on your way! I can't believe you. . . ."

"All right, Tam. Calm down." He put his arms around me and led me away from her. "Let's go in the waiting room and talk." "You wanna go?" he asked his father. The old man shook his head.

My legs felt wobbly beneath me. I had been sitting in

a hard plastic chair for several hours.

"Here, sit down at the table and I'll pour you some coffee."

"I don't want coffee!"

"You may not want it, little girl, but you sure as hell need it! Have you looked in a mirror lately?"

"I haven't been thinking of my appearance. I've been with Grandma constantly since the doctor called last Thursday."

"Nobody asked you to do that," he said, patronizing me.

"Are you suggesting that I shouldn't have come, that it isn't my place to be here?" I asked.

"Of course not!" He denied my accusation. "Well, not entirely anyway. I just don't understand why the doctor called *you*. The family left specific instructions at the desk as to whom to call, and when it was necessary to do so. Since your name isn't on the list, we're all a little confused as to how they ended up contacting the wrong person."

The wrong person.

For as long as I could remember I would hear his words. I had been *the wrong person!*

I stared at my father. He had not been part of my life since he'd divorced my mother and she had remarried. The man that my mother had married took care of my needs and treated me like I was his real daughter. I loved him deeply, but I could not erase the memories of another life with a different father. Only slowly had the unwelcome pictures of my birth father begun to fade. Not only did I never see him, but he never sent me a birthday card or made a phone call to see how my life was going. I had heard over and over again how he didn't have the decency to pay child support, let alone try and contact me. It wasn't until I was an adult—when his responsibility to provide those things for me ended—that he made any effort to have me back in his life. By that time, it was too late. Someone else had taken his place as my father, and I left it that way.

His mother was my only connection to my natural father's side of the family. Her affection for me had never waned.

Since I'd been the only one to visit her, the nurses were familiar with me. They knew I would come right away, so they had called me when she was comatose and close to death. Perhaps their compassion for a dying woman caused them to ignore the written orders barring all but immediate family, or maybe it was the fact that she'd asked for me.

My father could sense the anger and frustration bubbling up inside of me. His insinuation had callously ripped open old wounds of hate and rejection. Instead of rushing to his mother's side with concern over her condition, he chose to dispute the very fact of my presence.

"The wrong person!" I shouted at him. My chair flipped over backwards to the floor as I leapt to my feet in challenge to his accusation.

"I only meant. . . ."

"Don't bother explaining! I know exactly what you meant."

My anger continued to build as I moved closer to him to make my point. "Right from the beginning I begged you not to put her in this place. But no! You couldn't muster up the nerve to do what you and I both know was the right thing! Just as you couldn't face life with mother and left us. You allowed yourself to be pressured into this by people who don't care the least little bit about how Grandma wanted to spend the little time remaining to her life! I have been her only regular visitor since she was dumped here! And now you have the unmitigated gall to refer to me as the *wrong* person! How dare you!" I lunged toward him, thrusting my fist into his chest with all my might. A ferocious wave of tears burst forth out of my anguish.

"Tammy! Get hold of yourself!" he ordered.

What I was saying was true. He had succumbed to the rest of his family's wishes without even putting up a fight. In a way it wasn't his fault just as leaving us wasn't. He wanted only peace and harmony and no major confrontations. Nothing requiring guts or fortitude. He wasn't willing to stand alone to face what life brought and to stand the pain of doing what was right.

He was crying now, too. We stood there for a long time, both of us trying to understand one another. It was no use. The time had long passed for him to take his place as the pillar of strength in the family hierarchy. In my eyes, he was a coward now and forever.

I wept until my anguish eventually diminished to a hiccuplike sound.

"Are you going to be okay now?" he finally said.

"I think so."

"I didn't mean for things to turn out this way. You know that, don't you?"

"It doesn't matter anymore," I said softly.

"I'll stay with her now. You can go home and get some rest."

Was he serious? Did he really think I was just going to

leave Grandma after all these days? Emotions from the past, from the present filled me.

"No," I told him. "I'm not going to do that. I'm not going home. I need to stay here with her. If she wakes up and I'm not here, she'll. . . ."

"She's not going to wake up, Tam," he said. "Come here. I want you to see something." He took me by the arm and led me over to the mirror. "What do you see?"

I vaguely recognized the reflection of the woman staring back at me. Her skin was pale and cadaverous in appearance. Bloodshot eyes were sunk deep into their sockets encircled by rings of shadowy black. The bottom of her lip swelled with a line of blistering pustules. I ran my fingers over my face to see if it was really me. Indeed, it was. I had gone three days without sleep or food, the effects of which were having their revenge on my body. The spells were beginning again.

"I'm ill," I said.

My father brushed my words aside as he had my mother so long ago. "You're exhausted, Tam. You need to get some food in you and a good night's sleep."

I did look awful and I felt worse. The stomachaches and headaches were worsening. And those strange recurring sores I saw in the mirror were even more embarrassing. They used to be tiny thrushlike bumps. Now, in a matter of a day or two, they erupted into massive burning blisters. Sometimes the blisters spread uncontrollably to other parts of my body, down my neck and arms. I kept trying to stop them. Ointments, gels, astringents: I used them all in futile attempts to rid myself of the telltale signs. Nothing ever worked.

Maybe my father was right. I should go home to rest.

However, if there was even the slightest chance, the smallest hope that Grandma would return to us. . . . No, I knew that was not going to happen. Somehow, over the next few days, I needed to muster all the strength possible to face her death. I would have to put aside my distrust of my father to arrange the funeral.

"You'll call me if anything changes?"

"I promise."

He walked with me down the corridor. I stopped at Grandma's room for one last look. A peaceful shroud of serenity was on her face in that final moment between us.

There is nothing more you can do, I felt like she was saying. *The gifts I gave to you are tucked away in a special space within your heart. Love, courage, compassion—I gave them to you to guide you in my absence.*

I went home and for the first time in days slept soundly. The next day, however, the face my father had pointed out in the mirror looked worse, and my body felt weaker. I was in the midst of an attack.

Two days later we went to the funeral.

"It's time to close the casket now, Mr. Mundle," the man in the black silk suit told my father. "You should probably gather your family around for them to say their final farewells."

I didn't need to say goodbye. In my mind, Grandma wasn't really leaving. She wasn't in that long wooden box surrounded by brilliantly colored floral mounds at the front of the funeral parlor. Grandma was inside of me and I could feel her. She was helping me face these people, the ones who looked at me and felt contempt. They were all around me, surrounding me with their cruel accusations. My ears burned at the sound of their whispers. "Whatever possessed Mother to love such a person. Look at her!" The repulsion my father's relations displayed at my appearance was painfully evident each time they glared at me. But the sickness that was growing inside my body was increasingly becoming more powerful even than their contempt.

The sun began shining as we all got into our cars and headed for the burial site. Once there, we gathered around the casket being lowered into the ground. My stomach tightened in excruciating waves of pain and nausea as the minister read a last prayer. Thoughts banged furiously within my head, pounding at its walls to be released. The open sores that covered my face in a rashlike blanket were spreading to my torso and down my arms. My skin stung as though lye had been thrown on it. This was the worst attack I'd ever had. I tried to hide my pain from the others, but this time it wasn't possible. The sun beat down. My skin sizzled. I looked up.

"I can't see anything!" I screamed. Dizzy, I fell backwards towards the ground.

Tim's arms caught the force of my falling body. I shriveled in his embrace, becoming a lifeless, whimpering thing.

"Just get her out of here, Tim!" my father's annoyed voice commanded.

Tim maneuvered me past the throng of onlookers, their fingers pointing, their mouths dropping open in astonishment. I clung to him crying.

"How are you feeling, sweetheart?" Tim said brokenheartedly.

What else could he say? Tim had just witnessed the

most excruciating episode in my life, and he didn't have the power to make it better.

Finally we reached our car and Tim helped me in.

As we drove, the sky suddenly darkened and a blinding fury of rain splattered the windshield. It forced the wipers to swish rapidly against their attack. Tim drove cautiously down the disappearing blacktop. As the storm worsened, dividing his attention between the road and me was becoming increasingly difficult. I was broken, totally robbed of all that had been a nurturing source of comfort and continuance. Perhaps it was supposed to be like this, after all. Life is a series of births and deaths, events that we are expected to learn from in order to grow. But, was it supposed to hurt this much?

Tim said, "I've never seen your condition this bad before."

I nodded. A mysterious plague was ravaging my body with mad intensity. I wondered how he could look at me and still feel attracted to my swollen, ugly, disease-infested body.

"I've never felt worse, physically or emotionally," I said.

"I'll get you help. The best doctors. Whatever it takes. And we'll stay away from those awful people. You know, I just can't understand how your family could treat you that way! It really ticks me off!"

"It's always been this way. I guess I've just gotten used to it."

"Nobody, I don't care who they are, should have to get used to their family treating them that way."

"I guess you're right, but all I can cope with now is feeling this sick."

"This rain is really coming down, Tam. It's going to take us a long while to get home." He sighed. "Would you like to lie down in the back seat and get some rest?"

"No. I want to sit near you. My stomach hurts too much to sleep. I'll rest when I get home."

"Should I stop and buy you some antacid? Or, how about a soda? That always seems to settle your stomach."

"I'll be all right. Just keep driving. I want to get home and see the kids. I need to be with them; then everything will be better."

I curled my tired hurting body up against him and attempted to find a comfortable position. The children. They were my saving grace, my refuge in the storm of reality. My children had always been my reason to keep going. We had wanted to bring them with us, to say goodbye to Grandma. But, with all of the animosity, it seemed more prudent to have them stay home where they would be protected. Judging from the tumultuous events of the day, Tim and I had made the right decision.

To calm myself I envisioned what they were doing while they waited for us to return. Lori was starting supper, I thought. She was an excellent cook, no thanks to me. I was overjoyed when she showed an interest in the culinary arts. It was the one domestic duty that I had always viewed as a chore. Lori didn't see it as work because cooking was her passion in life. I only hoped the recurring headaches she'd been having lately hadn't returned.

I pictured Dan and Reuben in the living room, cheering on the Detroit Red Wings as they crushed their opponents. A littering rubble of popcorn bowls and soda cans surrounded them. I often wondered how Dan could seem to be doing several different things at once and actually be doing nothing at all.

Reuben was different. His attention was focused on each specific action. Doing any more than one or two things at once was confusing to him. He watched the game intently, memorizing each statistic, each instant replay. Reuben examined all of the players as their blades maneuvered across the ice, hoping to precisely reenact their strategies the next day with his own skates.

Johanna was not with the rest of them, I thought. She would be alone in her bedroom. Her inner sanctum was precious, a solitary refuge from the hectic pace of life. The soothing sounds of her playing the flute for hours came from behind the closed door. This was her passion. All other activities held no meaning for her. Sometimes I stopped what I was doing just to listen to her play, and it was enough. I had tried to understand her need for separation from the rest of us.

Regardless of how I imagined them enjoying their separate activities, I knew that they were all anxiously awaiting our return. Each child would occasionally glance out the window, hoping to catch a glimpse of our dark blue minivan bursting through the wall of falling rain. Storms of rain and snow were familiar to them; they had come to know them well. They were the same each winter, all winter. Likewise, they knew, with the bad weather it would take us longer than the usual three hours to make it home. Still, in their apprehension, they would wait, each of them silently uttering a prayer for our safe return.

Assuming the fetal position in the front seat of the car didn't seem to be diminishing my pain. It was an odd sensation, not quite nausea, not exactly cramping or burning. With each turn in the road, it increased. *Just a few more miles, just another hour or so and I will be home.*

I moved over and gripped the armrest with my hand as I waited silently for the pain to cease. I said nothing. Tim had enough to do without worrying any more over my condition.

Moving from one position to another, I tried to decrease the pain. Tim watched me from the corner of his eye. The expression on his face was one of alarm.

"Are you okay?"

I shook my head wearily. "No, I don't think so...this pain, it's getting worse."

"I'm going to find a drugstore in the next town and get you something. You're starting to scare me."

"Maybe you'd better. It's really getting bad. How far is Rogers City?"

"About ten miles. Can you hang on that long?"

I don't know. I closed my eyes. The intensifying pain was becoming unbearable. I felt like vomiting. A hard flaming knot burned inside my stomach, causing it to bloat up like a balloon. Lightheaded and dizzy, I felt everything spin in circles when my eyes flew open. I couldn't hold my nausea back anymore. Violent waves of dry heaves overcame me. With each rain-soaked mile in our path, they increased, finally taking control of my body.

I cried out, "Tim, don't bother with the drugstore." Another pain ripped at me. I stopped, barely able to catch my breath. "Just get me to the hospital!"

I could feel the jolt of the car as Tim stomped hard on the accelerator and turned toward help.

What was happening to me? Why was it happening?

Please, God, I can't stand it anymore. Please take it away. Make it all go away!

Chapter 8

The Darkest Night

Bolting through the large double doors of the emergency entrance, Tim carried me in his arms. "I need a doctor now!"

Several figures clothed in medical garb swarmed around us, directing Tim to a nearby examining room where he placed me gently on a stretcher.

A woman dressed in a white coat walked up to us. "I'm Dr. Carlton. What seems to be the problem?" she asked Tim.

His hand went to his forehead and wiped away the cold beads of perspiration. There was a look of confusion on his face. Confusion and fear.

"Sir, can you tell me what happened?"

"Yes, well. Not really. I mean, she's been sick off and on since before we met. Today we were at her grandmother's funeral when all of a sudden this pain came over her and she began to faint. I caught her."

Tim watched helplessly as the nurses removed my clothing and dressed me in a blue and white hospital gown.

"When did the vomiting start?"

"About half an hour ago. She hasn't been able to stop since she started," Tim said.

"Is she your wife?"

"Yes. Her name is Tammy. Tammy Evans."

"Has she been taking any kind of medication or have any medical problems that you are aware of? I've never seen anyone so unearthly pale"

"No, not that I know of." Tim shook his head, discounting the horrific, but apparently benign skin ailments I had since we met. "Please! Can you just help her? Give her something to make the pain go away?"

"It's going to be all right, Mr. Evans. We'll do our best," she reassured him. "I'm going to need you to fill out some paperwork at the front desk. You can come back and see your wife when you're finished. Don't worry. We'll try to find out what's going on with her," she said convincingly.

Tim went out to the lobby.

The doctor leaned over me, visually inspecting my condition as a nurse took my pulse.

"Doctor, her pulse is one forty!"

"Take it again!" the doctor ordered the nurse as she held a stethoscope to my chest.

"It's the same, Dr. Carlton."

"Mrs. Evans," the doctor yelled into my face. "Can you hear me? I'm Dr. Carlton. Do you know where you are?"

I struggled to reply, but could not find the strength to speak the words between each heave of my contracting stomach. I nodded my response to her, signaling that I understood.

"I need you to show me where the pain is."

There was no specific point or spot from which it had been emanating. My entire mid section writhed from its attack. Pointing to my lower torso was the best I could do.

"Mrs. Evans, I'm going to give you something for the pain and nausea. Are you allergic to any medications?" She was still yelling.

"No," I managed to whisper in desperate pain, forgetting my suspicions to the contrary.

"Is there a possibility that you might be pregnant?"

I shook my head no. I knew that I could not be pregnant because of the tubal ligation doctors had performed after Peter and I separated.

The white jackets continued to swarm at my bedside, speaking to each other in muffled tones that I could not comprehend. A large shiny needle pierced the skin of my left arm just above my wrist. I couldn't feel the sting of its puncture. I couldn't feel my arm at all. It was numb. A plastic bag hung over my head, dripping its clear fluid into my arm. Then, another needle punctured my hip. I felt the pressure of it, but not the sting.

"We're going to run some tests to find out what's causing your pain, Mrs. Evans. I need to do an ultrasound of your abdomen. The procedure doesn't hurt at all. Are you familiar with what an ultrasound is?"

I nodded to her again.

"I'll be right back with the machine. You just try to rest for a few minutes."

As she turned to leave the room, I struggled to speak. I wanted to know where my husband was. Why wasn't he with me? "Tim. . . ."

"Did you say something, Mrs. Evans?"

"My husband. Where . . . where is he?"

The excruciating pain and the ever increasing fear escalated. Thoughts collided together inside my head, interrupting the silence of the sterile room. The bright fluorescent light on the ceiling spun in nauseating circles, increasing my urge to vomit. A light tingling sensation raced up and down my limbs, my entire body quivering in response to its icy touch. I began retching. They brought a blue plastic pan and put it under my mouth. Finally, the vomiting subsided to an involuntary hiccup motion. A doctor watching called for an IV. Once it started, it worked swiftly. The pain was still there, but somehow I was beginning to feel less aware of it. My eyes attempted to focus on the blurred images in the room, but I couldn't. I was falling asleep. Not a deep peaceful sleep, but an absence of cognizance of the world around me.

A shadowy figure entered the room, uttering jumbled phrases at me. I couldn't understand what she was saying. It was as though she were speaking in a foreign language. Others came into the room quickly, clustering together in an unrecognizable mass. They mouthed their words in slow motion, just inches from my face, the tone of their voices commanding a response.

One shook me. I reacted like a straw doll. "You need to wake up, Mrs. Evans! You're having a reaction to the medication!"

"She's not responding, Doctor."

"Mrs. Evans. *TAMMY!* If you don't come around, we'll have to give you a drug to counteract the pain medication!"

"Pulse is over one seventy-five. BP is at. . . ."

Their voices trailed off, moving further and further away from me. I liked the place where I was. There was no pain there, no violent waves of nausea. I had floated off to a flourishing oasis in a desert of affliction. Their pleas for me to return to them held no significance. I didn't want to go back. There was pain and suffering where they were. Only contentment and serenity occupied this new reality, where the darkness of existence held no fear. . . .

I opened my eyes. Tim's masculine frame became increasingly clearer through the foggy mist.

Morning sunlight streamed through the hospital window blinds, casting iridescent prisms on the clean white wall of the hospital room. The snowstorm was gone, its lingering remnants melting off the roof of the building in sparkling, pencil-thin streams. After a cursory inspection, I noticed that the pain had also disappeared, leaving nothing but fatigue and weakness in its stead.

"Thank God, you're back, darling. I was afraid you might have left me for good!" The softness of his voice was comforting to me.

"Don't worry, Tim, I wouldn't leave you here alone to squander our children's inheritance. That's *my* job!"

Tim chuckled at my statement with a sense of relief in his voice. "Now I know you're feeling better!"

"What happened?" I asked, still groggy from being asleep for so long.

"Well, they're not really sure. You definitely had an allergic reaction to the pain medication they gave you. But, as far as what caused all this to begin with, they're still trying to figure that out. Dr. Carlton is supposed to come in this morning to see how you're doing. She said the results from the testing would be in by then."

"I feel like I've been run over by a truck! I guess I look like it, too."

"Actually, you don't look that bad, compared to yesterday. The rash seems to be beginning to heal and the color is coming back into your face. Besides, you'll always be beautiful to me, no matter what."

He placed my hand in his own, gently kissing the tiny gold laced diamonds and rubies in my wedding band. Tim had stayed at my bedside all night, keeping vigil over me. He looked exhausted, his big brown eyes swollen and bloodshot from crying. He leaned forward to scrutinize me better.

"Darling. Everything's fine. See! I'm better. I'm just a little weak, that's all."

"I was just so scared! I can't even imagine going on without you."

"Well, I'm not about to let that happen, so just put those thoughts right out of your head."

From the fearful look on his face, Tim needed consolation. We had taken this dark journey together, each of us experiencing entirely different yet deeply intense pain. He had been my rock, my pillar of stability and now it was my turn to be there for him.

"I love you, Tim. Try not to worry. We're going to beat this." I tried to make my words sound more certain than my thoughts were.

He smiled.

Then I thought of the children. We had to tell them something or they'd be frightened.

"Did you call the kids and tell them that I'm in the hospital?"

"I talked to Lori last night and told her you were in the

hospital and had some weird kind of flu. They're all worried, of course, but Lori said she would keep things under control until we came back. I'm supposed to call her again this morning and let her know how you're doing."

"Please call her back. I don't like them being alone for this long."

"It isn't even seven o'clock, Tam. I'm sure they're all still in bed."

"Please, Tim! I'm going to lie here and worry about them if you don't."

"All right, if it will make you happy. If nobody's up, I'll just leave a message on. . . ."

The door to the hospital room cracked ajar. "Good morning! I hope I'm not interrupting anything." Dr. Carlton sounded both surprised and relieved that I was awake and coherent. "You must be feeling a lot better than you did yesterday, Mrs. Evans."

"Yes, I am, thank you. Sorry for giving you such a scare."

"Oh, that's okay. I could use a little shaking up now and then. It keeps me on my toes! I'm just happy to see that you're feeling better. Are you in any pain?"

"No, just tired."

"Mrs. Evans, has anything like this ever happened to you before? I'm still a bit puzzled over your symptoms."

"Well, I have had that same pain before, but never quite so intense. I've had these sores on and off all my life, but they've never been this bad, either."

"Have you ever been treated for any of these symptoms?"

"Some." I told her some of the diagnoses I'd received

and how none of the medication had ever helped. "I usually just wait it out."

Looking puzzled, Dr. Carlton leafed through the pages of my file. It was obvious she had no idea what was wrong with me. All she could do was guess. "I noticed that you have a rather long jagged scar on your lower right abdomen. Is that from an appendectomy?"

I had completely forgotten about that. It was so long ago, when I was a teenager. Yes, it was the same pain, and I'd had the same sores!

"I had my appendix removed when I was about twelve. The extra scarring is from all the time I had to be reopened because of a staph infection. I had to be on antibiotics a long time. For a while, my parents didn't think I was going to make it. You don't think that could have anything to do with what's happening now, do you?"

"I'm not sure, and I don't think it would be wise for me to even speculate."

"Well, what do you think happened to me yesterday?"

She looked apprehensive, but she had to give me some kind of answer.

"For now I am going to suggest and, mind you, it is a suggestion not a diagnosis, that what you experienced was a kidney stone."

Tim and I couldn't believe what we were hearing. Our mouths dropped open simultaneously in skepticism. Dr. Carlton could tell by our shell-shocked expressions that we weren't going to buy such a ridiculous explanation.

"Just hear me out. Between the ultrasound and the manifestation of pain and its intensity, it sounds very much like a kidney stone. The skin rash? I don't know. It's probably an entirely different problem altogether. I'm going to write you a prescription for an antibiotic. When you get home, I want you to make an appointment with your family doctor. While you're there, ask him about the rash. He'll probably refer you to a dermatologist."

She wrote out the prescription quickly in her embarrassment, handing it to Tim before turning to leave.

"That's it? I mean, you're just going to send her home?" Tim asked, wanting her to do more for me.

"Your wife is fine now, Mr. Evans. She doesn't need to be in the hospital. The kidney stone should pass within a day or two."

Abruptly, Dr. Carlton left the room. It was almost as if she didn't believe her own words and was finding it difficult convincing us to believe them. I definitely *didn't* believe her.

My physical pain was gone. Now, confusion reigned, dictating its power over my thoughts. What was happening to my body? Where could I go to find comfort for my shattered resistance?

"Home," Tim said.

"I will take you there and when you're inside it with all of us I know you will feel better. I'll go call the kids now."

From the moment we pulled into the driveway, I felt a release of the anxiety that had been penned up inside the past few days. A freshly carved path through the blanket of newly fallen snow led the way to the front steps. The warm glow of lamplight emanated from the beveled glass window panes of the enormous Victorian structure. Ours was the largest home on the block, one we had all worked hard to restore. I had fallen in love with the house from the instant

I saw it. It needed us, a family whose laughter and tears could comfort its inner walls. We nursed it back to health, back to its original proud grandeur, one room at a time. Now it was a part of us, a haven of peace and safety against the storms of life in the outside world. It felt so good to be home!

Inside, my four children gathered round me all at once. I tried to appear normal to them, as if nothing had happened, but it was no use. Their individual expressions of frightened concern told me they saw through my charade. They gawked in silence at my hunched-over stature, at the blistering rash that covered my arms and face. Turning to Tim for an explanation, they saw in his eyes a look that said now was not the time to ask. They obeyed his unspoken command, devoting their collective attention to making me as comfortable as possible.

"Here, Mom, come lay down on the sofa," Lori said. "I'll be right back with a blanket and your pillow."

"I'll fix you a cup of hot cocoa." Johanna's golden hair bounced behind her as she hurried toward the kitchen to complete the task.

Dan and Reuben brought in our luggage. They weren't sure what more they could say to make me feel better, other than the occasional "I love you, Mom," each time they passed me.

Each rushed through their appointed duties in order to rejoin me at my makeshift bedside. They didn't ask questions about the funeral or the night in the hospital. Instead, a fluttering narrative of their own events of the past two days came from them. Their sports scores and general happenings tangled together confusing my already wandering thoughts, further weakening my exhausted mind and body.

"Okay, guys. We'd better give Mom some time alone to sleep. She's had a rough couple of days. Let's go in the kitchen."

Tim cleared the room, kissing my forehead before excusing himself. "Don't worry about a thing. Just concentrate on getting better and we'll take care of everything else."

It sounded simple enough, but was it really possible? Even with rest, a lot of it, was I ever going to feel better again? I heard them talking behind the swinging shutters at the entrance to the kitchen, bombarding their questions at Tim.

"What's happening?"

"Why does Mom look so bad?"

"What did the doctor say was wrong with Momma?"

He had no answers, no specific answers. Instead, Tim tried to explain as best he could the events which had taken place. Gradually, I fell asleep to the static of their whispers, hoping to wake again with the knowledge that my suffering had just been a bad dream.

Sometime later—I would never have guessed an entire night had passed—I awoke to find Tim at my bedside and the house quiet.

"Where did everyone go?"

"It's all right, Hon. You slept through the night. It's almost nine o'clock. The kids went off to school about an hour ago. I told them to be quiet and let you sleep. How are you feeling?"

That was a good question, yet one I was not fully awake enough to respond to intelligently. A cursory inspection told me there was no stomach pain and I felt more refreshed than I had in a long time. Suddenly, a twinge of panic raced through me, the kind of panic that strikes when you feel like you may have missed something important.

"What day is it?" I begged of Tim.

"It's Monday morning. Why?"

I pushed back the blanket, trying to get up. "I can't lay around all morning. I have to be at work at ten o'clock! Why didn't you wake me up sooner?" I struggled to my feet.

Tim caught me in his arms as my body collapsed. A sharp pain stabbed me in the middle of my back, just between the shoulder blades, as he helped me to the sofa.

"Hold on a minute! You just sit yourself right back down! I've already called the store and told your boss you weren't coming in today."

"But I have to! I've never missed a day. . . ."

"I know, I know, but you're in no condition to go anywhere, except maybe back to the hospital."

I began to weep. "But. . . ."

"Now, not another word about it! Look, I picked up your prescription and I want you to take it. Then you can call and make yourself a doctor's appointment later this afternoon. I have to go to work. Now, I'll be home around three o'clock and I can take you then."

His words made me feel like one of the children. Yet, I knew he was right. My head was still spinning, and the newly apparent stabbing pain was getting worse.

"I'm not trying to be mean, honey. You know that, don't you? I just want you to be well again."

I washed down two of the large pink tablets with the water he handed me. Dr. Carlton had suggested that I see my family doctor. Now, feeling so terrible, I had no choice.

"All right! I give in! Besides, I'm in a lot of pain and I'd like to know what's really going on."

"Is it the same pain as before?"

"No, it's in my back now. I just noticed it when I stood up."

"I think I'd better stay home from work and keep an eye on you," Tim said as he reached for the phone.

"Don't be silly . . . I'll be fine. Both of us can't afford to miss a day's work over this. I promise, I'll call the doctor and you can take me there when you get home. I'm going to take a shower and lie down on the sofa until you come back. Okay?"

Tim hesitated. He looked worried, worried that I was not telling him how bad it really was.

"You're sure?"

"Yes, I'm sure. Now, go on. Get out of here before you're late!"

Tim left the house, still feeling apprehensive. I stood up slowly this time, holding onto furniture as I headed toward the bathroom for my shower. The pain that had started out as a minor annoyance was beginning to resemble the one I'd felt just days before. I was scared! Holding onto the shower walls for stability, I didn't know if the trembling in my hand was from weakness or if it was a brand new symptom.

By the time Tim and the children came home, I was curled into a ball on the couch in intense agony. My body cringed tensely at even the slightest touch. The skin itself seemed to burn whenever I moved or my clothing rubbed against it. It was clearly apparent that, whatever was wrong with me, was more than just a kidney stone. The pain seemed located in my spine, branching out in every direction from it. Moving or stretching didn't cause the pain to increase. It just made it more apparent. I felt dizzy and nauseous whenever I moved my head.

I made an appointment with our family physician, Dr. Conroy, for two-thirty the next day. Tim came home from work to drive me there. The doctor took x-rays and checked me over, but like everyone else he was unable to locate the source or cause of what was debilitating me.

"The x-rays were normal, Tammy. The blood test and urinalysis were normal, too. I can't find anything wrong with you physically from my exam, either."

"But, how could that be?"

"You said you've had been under a lot of stress lately. The body can do funny things when you're stressed out. I'm going to give you a prescription and I want you to take it for the next couple of weeks."

"Dr. Carlton, in Rogers City, said I had a reaction to the pain medication she gave me. It isn't the same one, is it?"

"I don't know what she gave you, but I can call and find out. I doubt that it's the same. This is a muscle relaxer with few side effects, if any."

"What about the kidney stone?"

"Well, you may have had one, but it seems unlikely. If you want, I can refer you to a specialist, but I really don't think it's necessary."

"No, that's all right. I trust your judgment."

"I want you to go home and get some rest. It's the best thing for you right now. If you're not better in a week or so, give me a call."

With that, he was gone, leaving me even more confused and frustrated than I had been before. There was something sinister going on inside my body! It wasn't stress or a kidney stone, or both. And, what about the rash? He didn't even notice it. Or, if he had, it wasn't important enough for him to mention.

Tim stopped at the drug store on our way home. I took the medication he picked up, but it didn't work. If anything, the pain increased. By the next morning it had expanded to a nearly intolerable level. It was all I could do to pull myself out of bed and walk down the stairs. My body swayed back and forth as if I was suffering a drunken stupor. I was losing control. My equilibrium and my vision during the day were growing noticeably worse.

"I'm sorry, son. I didn't mean to bump into you."

"My fault, Mom," Dan said.

"Where are you off to?"

"School." Dan had a strange look on his face, wondering why I would even ask such an absurd question. He was going to the place he went to every weekday morning, of course. Dan had his trombone case in one hand and his backpack slung over his shoulder. It should have been totally obvious where he was off to.

"Mom? Are you okay?"

"Yes, of course. I'm fine! Where is everyone else?"

"They already left, Mom. Dad had an early meeting. He said not to wake you up. Look, Mom." He glanced at his watch. "It's seven forty-five, and I'll be late for the bus."

"Well, you'd better get going then!"

Dan held onto my arm gently.

"Mom?"

"Really, Dan. I'm fine. Just a little tired is all."

I sat down at the kitchen table with his assistance.

"Should I call Dad?"

"C'mon now, Dan! All I need is a cup of coffee to

wake me up a bit more."

"Well, if you say so. I really gotta go, Mom."

I could see he didn't want to leave me in that condition, so I sat up taller in the chair, forcing a slight
smile. It took all my strength to cover up what was happening inside me, hiding my trembling hands tightly
together under the tablecloth so he could not see them.

"Have a good day, son. I'll see you after school."

"Mom?"

"Yes?"

"I love you."

The door slammed behind him, and I watched through
the window as he ran out to the street to wait. I could let go
now. As I drew them from under the table, my hands shook
uncontrollably in front of me. I stared at them in disbelief
and fear. *What was happening to me?* I drew my quivering
hands to my face, tracing over the places where the rash had
been. It was nearly gone, the texture of my skin feeling
smooth to the touch. But now, other things had come to take
its place. I wasn't sure which was worse, the cutting pain in
the middle of my back, or these new problems which seemed
to have come on while I slept.

Cautiously, I trudged over to the counter and reached
for the coffeepot. I carefully poured the piping hot brew from
the spout, only spilling a drop. With both hands wrapped
around the cup, I slowly shuffled back to the table, focusing
all my effort on getting the hot brew there safely. Tremors
moved quickly down my arms and into my hands and fingers
like an electrical pulse. In an involuntary reaction, the cup
jumped out of my hands, smashing onto the ceramic tile.
Boiling hot liquid splattered over the cabinet doors and

dripped down the front of my housecoat. I didn't even scream. I stood in the kitchen, staring at the broken shards floating in the steamy brown puddle on the floor.

Anger! Not fear or frustration, but anger now encompassed me. Something strange and uninvited was attempting to overpower my will, and it was succeeding. I had no way to stop it! I clenched my fists into tight defiant balls, raising them. *"Why are you doing this to me? Why are you allowing this to happen!"*

No one answered. My anger at those who were ignoring my pleas for help burst forth in a wave of resentful tears, casting my body onto the floor in a limp, crumpled heap next to the mess I had made. My hope was gone, ripped away by the nameless force that now took possession of me. There was nothing left to do but cry!

When I got hold of myself I inched to the phone and dialed my doctor's number. Luckily he was in.

"It's getting worse, Dr. Conroy. My hands and arms are shaking constantly. My eyes are burning and my face is kind of numb on the right side. I'm really starting to get scared!"

The voice on the other end of the phone had a puzzled tone to it. "I want you to stop taking the medication I gave you. It doesn't seem to be helping and it may very well be causing the numbness and tremors."

"But I thought you said it wouldn't cause any side effects!"

"Normally it wouldn't. But you seem to have a low tolerance for any kind of medication. I don't know, Tammy. I'm a general practitioner. These symptoms are a little out of my area of expertise. I think you need to see an orthopedic surgeon."

"A *what*?"

"I'm thinking that you may have an inflamed disc or something that is pinching a nerve in your spine. That could be causing all your neurological symptoms. I'm sorry, Tammy, that's the best I can come up with. I still think your problem's stress related. All of the tests showed there is nothing physically wrong with you."

I hung up the phone, dejected.

The days dragged on, one agonizing hour after the other. *There is nothing physically wrong with you* played over and over in my head, like a static-riddled recording. I stayed in my room, in my bed, where my family could not see me and become as frightened as I was. They left me alone to rest, but that wasn't making me any better. I felt worse. The thought that I might actually be going crazy crossed my mind more than once.

"Your mom is on the phone, hon. Do you want me to tell her to call back later?" Tim smoothed my hair lovingly.

I pulled myself out from under the comforter, shielding my eyes from the daylight. "No. I can talk to her."

I picked up the phone from the nightstand, the receiver jumping around uncontrollably in my hand.

"Are you doing any better, Tam?"

"No, Mom, I'm not. It seems to be getting worse, not better."

"Well, listen. I had lunch with the Pastorellis today after church and told them what was going on. Dr. Pastorelli said he wants to examine you. He'll see you today if you want."

"Mom, Dr. Pastorelli is an eye doctor. What could he possibly do for me?"

"I don't know, but your vision's getting worse and he felt that might be a clue. It's worth a try, Tam. Nothing else is working."

My mother and stepfather picked me up an hour later and drove me to Dr. Pastorelli's office.

He examined my eyes, one at a time. The brightness from his penlight burned my eyes even more, causing a blinding, stinging sensation.

"Now, with your eyes closed, I want you to raise your arms straight out in front of you and walk over to me."

I did my best, trying not to fall over. Closing my eyes made the nausea worse. My hands fluttered in a chaotic sequence in the air. It felt like the room was spinning faster and faster with each step I took. Before I could make it even halfway to where he was standing, I lost my balance entirely, falling against the metal instrument table. It was no use. I clung tightly to my mother's hand and she helped me back to the chair.

"There is definitely some neurological damage. I can see that. What is causing it? That is what I don't know right now. I want you to see a neurologist I know in Petoskey. He's very good and I can probably get you in right away."

I sighed and tears rose to my eyes, "So I'm not going crazy, after all? There really is something physically wrong with me?"

The doctor laughed heartily at my comment. "The one thing of which I'm quite sure is that you are not crazy, Tammy! There *is* something wrong, but you're going to have to be examined by a neurologist to find out what it is." Dr. Pastorelli left the room to make the phone call.

"This is really getting scary, Mom. I can't imagine what kind of neurological problem I could have, can you?" I studied her face. "Is this anything like the problems you have with your multiple sclerosis? Do you think I could have it, too?"

She shook her head vehemently. "Believe me, if your symptoms were like mine I would have told you. But they're nothing like what I have. Be glad about that. And don't worry. This neurologist friend of Dr. Pastorelli's will find out what's wrong." She turned away.

The doctor came back into the room and handed me a slip of paper with the name and phone number of the doctor at Wyatt's Clinic.

"He can't see you today. I'm getting nothing but his answering machine. Here is his number. Call there in the morning and tell the office manager I referred you and that I said you need to be seen as soon as possible. Until then, I want you to go home and rest."

Go home and rest. It was the same thing I had been advised to do by everyone else, and it wasn't making me feel any better. Did I have a fatal disease or a malignant tumor or what? Such possibilities frightened me even more. The only option I had left was to follow Dr. Pastorelli's instructions and keep the appointment with the specialist. Perhaps this new doctor would have the answers I was searching for. Perhaps this was the one who would be able to find out what was wrong with me.

Chapter 9

Broken Silence

The young neurologist was a tall, blond, lean man, very kind and gentle. He examined me in his office for over an hour. By the time he had tapped my knees and poked my skin lesions at many different locations he appeared just as perplexed as the other doctors I had seen. Dr. Ratliff could find nothing wrong with me either, and decided to admit me to the hospital for further testing.

He buzzed for an attendant who took me to my room. Then a bouncy red-haired nurse came in to take down my medical history. Before asking me any information, she picked up the hospital gown and dangled it in front of me. "Now, Mrs. Evans, I know it's not exactly the latest fashion, but you're going to have to put this on."

I had left it folded neatly at the foot of the bed, hoping to avoid wearing it at all. Not only was it ugly, just as in the past, but now it signified something dreadful to me. There were sick people all around me, moaning in their beds, hooked up to tubes and machines. If I put on the gown, I would become one of them. I was sure wearing that blue-and-white-striped costume would only make me sicker than I already was. There was even the chance that I would never be well again, that I would never leave the hospital—if I put it on.

"C'mon, hon. It's only for a day or two. The sooner you put the gown on, the sooner they can do their tests and you can go home," Tim pointed out.

Behind the drawn curtain, Tim helped me change out of my jeans and sweatshirt and into the dreaded hospital garb. He had been helping me for days to get in and out of my clothes, as I could no longer do it on my own. My fingers didn't have the strength to tug at zippers or buttons. Even if they did, their trembling would not allow me to grasp the apparatus and finish dressing. Now Tim tied the frayed white strings in the back of the gown and I shuffled to the bed, exhausted from the experience.

"That's much better," the nurse said, very upbeat. "Now we can get on with the rest of it."

Her questions tired me further. I tried to concentrate, telling her as much as I could remember about my family's medical history. I didn't know much. I wasn't aware of any medical problems on my father's side. And, as far as I knew, my mother was the only one on her side of the family with any health problems.

"Mom was often ill and I always asked her what it was. She told me she had multiple sclerosis and some other problems, but what, I don't know," I told the nurse, trying to convey the mystery involved. "I know there were times when she had a lot of trouble with her legs. They would swell up and she would have difficulty walking, but then it would go away. My mother hid her bouts with illness as well as she could, for she was a proud woman and never wanted to inflict her suffering on anyone else. Whenever she became ill, she would hide in her bedroom until it was over." The thought passed through my mind that I had been doing the same thing lately. "Anyway, the disease that made my mother retreat to her bedroom seems to be growing worse as mother spends more time incapacitated."

The nurse's questions were becoming too difficult for me to answer. My head pounded as I realized the secrecy surrounding my mother's "bad times" would not satisfy the nurse. I didn't want to think about those times.

"That's all right, Mrs. Evans. I'll come back tomorrow. I'm sure we'll be feeling better by then and we can talk some more."

She bounced out of the room, but the headache stayed with me, making my head feel like it was going to explode. I realized that I hadn't eaten anything of any significance in days and hadn't had anything at all since the night before. Tim went down to the vending machine and brought back a couple of candy bars. I wolfed them down, not caring if they came right back up again.

The CAT scan was first. It too showed nothing. Next, they did an MRI.

As I lay on the table, they slid my body headfirst into a cylinder. It seemed like it was no more than a couple of inches from my face. Being in such a closed-in space reminded me of a coffin. I became even more nauseous. After a few minutes I was able to calm down and realized I wasn't going to be locked there forever! It's remarkable what a person can do when there are no alternatives. I closed my eyes. The music piped into the tube was somewhat soothing, so I did my best to concentrate on that. Every half hour or so they would let me back out for a few minutes, while the films were checked. After two hours, it was over. The technicians were kind and allowed me to look at the films with them. I was amazed at the quality and clarity of the images. I couldn't see anything out of the ordinary on those films. My intuition was confirmed shortly after returning to the room.

"The MRI results were negative, too," Dr. Ratliff said.

"What does that mean?" I asked.

"It means that we haven't found the right test yet, Mrs. Evans. I want to do one more. If that turns up negative, well, I don't know what else we can do."

"There has been someone here from the lab drawing blood, two, sometimes three times a day. Haven't any of those tests shown anything?"

"No, unfortunately they haven't." I could sense his growing frustration. "You've had every kind of blood test imaginable, and nothing has turned up positive. Are you *sure* you aren't feeling any better?"

"No, I'm not."

He looked at me searchingly. I could tell he didn't believe me, but it was the truth. "In fact, it's getting worse. Now my legs are beginning to feel funny, like they're asleep."

"Well," he said with a rather perturbed tone. "I have no choice but to perform a lumbar puncture."

I didn't know what "performing a lumbar puncture" consisted of but, by the expression on his face, I knew it wasn't going to be fun. It was almost like he was trying to scare me into being well.

"What is that?" I asked.

"You know, a spinal tap. I'll have to draw several vials of fluid from your spine and have them analyzed for disease."

"Do you *have* to do it?"

"It's the only test you haven't had yet. If you *really* want to find out what's wrong with you, then, yes, I'm going to have to do it." I felt he was hoping I would decline the offer.

"Well then, let's get it over with!"

Dr. Ratliff looked startled at my response. It obviously was not the one he was expecting. I could tell that he didn't believe I was sick at all, that I had either made it all up or it was just like all the other doctors had suggested—stress.

After gathering all the necessary equipment and two technicians, he instructed me to sit on the edge of the bed and lean my body over the bed table. He proceeded to give me a local anesthetic in the lower portion of my back. In the few minutes it took for the anesthetic to take effect, he began explaining what the procedure entailed. As he explained it to me, a dreadful dark cloud of helplessness came over me. I couldn't even fathom what he was telling me was about to occur. My body froze as my mind raced around in circles.

"Stay absolutely still so I can insert the needle without incident," he said. First, I felt a mild amount of pressure until the needle punctured the spinal column. Then there was an explosion inside my body. By instinct, I jumped back. Luckily, so did he! After a few seconds of calming down for both of us, he continued by withdrawing the spinal fluid. A tingling began in my limbs and then there was almost an instant loss of feeling in both legs. Within seconds my heart began pounding violently and loud bells rang in my ears. Sweat flowed out in streams from every pore in my body. The nausea of the past few days was now out of control and

I knew I was going to throw up.

"I can't stand anymore. I'm going to be sick!"

"You're going to have to wait until I'm finished to throw up!" he shouted at me. Then he said to the attendants, "Hold her down."

Keeping under control for the next five minutes was one of the most difficult tasks I had ever been forced to accomplish. With a deep breath and eyes closed, I envisioned my children in my mind's eye. One by one, I concentrated on them and how much I loved them. It allowed me to tune the scene out and that was desperately required in this situation.

I managed to repress the urge to vomit until the needle was out. While the nurse helped me clean up, Dr. Ratliff instructed me on the importance of lying perfectly still for the next four hours so as not to experience the severe headache some people suffer after a lumbar procedure.

"I don't think that will be a problem," I whispered as the nurse pulled the covers up over me. The energy was entirely drained from my body, like a dead battery.

Before leaving the room with the six vials of spinal fluid, he showed them to me. "Well, they're clear," he said. "That's a good indication we won't find anything here either. I'll be back in a few hours with the results. I'll call in your husband. He's waiting outside."

Tim pulled a chair up to the side of the bed and stroked my arm until I fell asleep. At seven o'clock that evening, the doctor returned. I had been asleep, dead asleep, for more than eight hours.

When I woke up, my mother and dad were there. It was evident they had been at the hospital for quite some time. Mom and Tim stood next to my bed, chatting quietly.

Dad was perched in front of the television set, watching CNN. I sat up slowly, still heeding the doctor's warning concerning the headache.

"There is nothing wrong with you, Mrs. Evans. The lumbar puncture was negative, just as I had suspected. I'm going to release you. You can go home tonight."

"Just wait a second, here!" Tim exploded. "My wife has been sick for weeks now. Since she's been in this hospital, she's gotten worse, right before your eyes! She can barely walk, or use her arms, and the pain . . . the pain is unbearable! And now, you're telling us there's nothing wrong with her?"

"That's exactly what I'm saying. Your wife is perfectly healthy, Mr. Evans. At least, *physically* anyway."

I burst out in tears as they fought over me as if I wasn't even in the room. Mom and Dad put their arms around Tim, trying to calm him down. He was the only one that had witnessed all my suffering from the outset. He knew I hadn't been faking any of the symptoms. How could I? They were real, and we both knew it. The suggestion that it was all psychological was deeply hurtful, especially when I thought about the accusations at Grandma's funeral. When no easy scientific answer could be found, doctors and laymen alike blamed the victim.

Mother brushed her hair from her eyes and turned to me. Her look was one of horror.

She spoke in a low voice. "Dr. Ratliff, I have porphyria. I recently found out that it can be inherited. Can you check Tammy for the disease?"

Dr. Ratliff's eyes popped wide open in astonishment, as did his mouth. He stared at my mother with a confused look. "I've heard of that...I think...I mean," he began haltingly. Then he stopped.

His shock was undoubtedly related to the fact that I had not mentioned my mother's illness to him or anyone, but how could I?! My own mother, that long suffering woman—had she hurt this way all her life? Was this unheard of illness, so rare that no one had thought to test me for it, the reason...she had climbed up to her room one afternoon not to return for nearly half a year?

"What makes you *think* you have porphyria? Who diagnosed you?" he asked, his voice deeper now. I could tell he was more than hesitant to believe either one of us by now.

As ghosts of the past swirled around me, my mother answered the doctor in a stern voice: "I don't *think* I have porphyria, Dr. Ratliff. I *know* I do!" The doctor had met his match in my mother. "I was diagnosed at the University of Michigan Medical Center by Dr. Cohen. But, since he passed away, I've been under the care of Dr. Stewart at Wyatt's Clinic."

Dr. Ratliff turned pale. Obviously there was a new sense of urgency to the situation, an urgency I was not alert enough to fully comprehend. Though I was still in a fog from sleeping so long, even I could see the surprise and confusion which set in at the suggestion of this *porphyria*, of which I never heard before.

"And what is your name?" Dr. Ratliff took a pen out of his pocket and waited for my mother's response.

"Judy. Judy Taracks. If you call Dr. Stewart at Wyatt's he has all the information about me in his files."

"I'm going to make a phone call right now, and I'll be back." The doctor's voice trailed off as he ran down the hall to the nurses' station.

I looked over at my mother, astonished.

"Why in the world didn't you tell me I could have

porphyria? I always thought you had multiple sclerosis! I just can't believe you didn't say anything about it all the times I asked you if my disease could be the same as yours."

"How could I know?" she said sadly. "Our symptoms are so different. And no one ever told me my type of porphyria could be inherited. But the other day I mentioned your illness to Dr. Stewart and how no one could diagnose what it was and that's when he told me that some research suggests a genetic component for some types of porphyria, including my kind."

I felt bewildered. "What do you mean, your kind? Is there more than one kind of porphyria?"

"Yes, Tammy, apparently there is."

"This whole time I've been thinking that the reason I was sick had something to do with multiple sclerosis. And now you're telling me that you think it could be porphyria. Why didn't you say something to me about it?"

"I wanted to," she said. "But I thought I should wait until after the test results came back. I guess I was just scared to even imagine that you could have porphyria as well as me. It's too awful to contemplate. You don't know what it's like." She shuddered.

It was too much, all that my mother was telling me. We were both crying now. She put her hand on my forehead, rubbing it with soft gentle strokes. "It's going to be all right. At least the doctor can check it out. I pray what you have is different."

I stared at her. Did she realize what she had done by keeping the intricacies of her illness a secret all these years? I couldn't tell what she felt. I had enough to deal with just figuring out what *I* was feeling about this discovery. But I had always seen my mother, despite her sick periods, as strong and resilient. Now I was seeing something contrary about her. She was scared to death! She had kept a terrible secret even when not revealing it could have caused serious, even fatal repercussions for me and I could see, by her frightened expression and the tears she was unable to conceal, that she now understood what a dangerous thing she had done.

Dr. Ratliff flew back into the room within minutes. He was carrying a large plastic container. Over the past three days I had watched his demeanor go from kind to skeptical and then to humble. "After speaking with your mother's doctor, I've decided to take a twenty-four-hour urine collection from you, Tammy. The urine will then have to be sent to a research hospital in Minnesota for testing. It will be a week or so before we know anything.

"You're going to have to stay in the hospital for at least another twenty-four hours," he told me.

I didn't want to stay there another minute! The part of me that hurt the most right now was my heart. I missed my children so much! I missed the smell of their familiar, individual scents, the laughter of their impish spirits. My arms ached to hold them. We had never spent this much time away from each other and I knew they would be frightened.

However, I knew there was no way I was going to talk anyone into letting me get out of there. Mom and Dad left only after I promised I wouldn't try to escape. Tim went home shortly afterward. He was as confused and afraid as I was. He loved my mother and knew she was often ill, but, like me, he attributed it to multiple sclerosis. While the doctors whom I had consulted always came up with some plausible explanation for each individual ailment I suffered, I didn't think it had ever occurred to any of them to look at all of the symptoms to see if they were related. With the bewilderment Tim was experiencing, it was a wonder he was able to run back and forth between the children and me, taking care of all of us. Maybe it was good he was so busy. He wouldn't have time to think about what he had gotten himself into by marrying into my family!

I was released from the hospital the following evening and Tim picked me up. I left knowing no more about my physical condition than when I first arrived, except that now I was waiting for the results of the porphyria test. The only thing that I was sure of was that the disease was getting worse. I was becoming weaker and more symptomatic. The nausea came on almost the instant I walked out the hospital doors. The lights from the oncoming cars stung my eyes and with my thoughts about Mother, I had an uncomfortable two-hour trip. "Tim," I said as soon as we were alone, "I still can't fathom how my mother could have kept the fact that she had porphyria from me."

"I can't either," he said. "You need to have this out with her."

"You know I can't," I said sadly. " I have to believe she is suffering even more than I am over this revelation."

"I guess she is, but that doesn't relieve her of the responsibility for not disclosing her disease."

Being able to go home and kiss my children, reassuring each of them I was going to be all right, made all the horror of the previous few days begin to fade into memory.

I realized being in my own home with my family

around me was the best medicine. I prayed the test would be
negative and this would all be behind us. I hugged each one
of my children, never wanting to let them go again.

Tim looked at the messages on the phone table. "Your
brother called a little while ago. He said he wanted to drive
over for the day and see how you're doing. He's bringing
Chelene and Caroline." Tim added softly, "I hope that's okay."

Tim wasn't sure whether or not I wanted any visitors.
I was feeling worse than when I had left the hospital. Each
hour that passed I became weaker as the pain and multitude
of ever-changing symptoms became stronger.

To my surprise, I realized my feelings were the same
as my mother's. Like her, I didn't want other people to view
me as a pathetic invalid. Once again, Tim helped me to put
on some more appropriate clothes than the sweatsuit I'd
worn home and then I went into the bathroom and struggled
through putting on some makeup. I had never seen my skin
look so white. It was almost unearthly, like a vampire's:

Tammy, Tammy skin so white,

You're a creature of the night.

Seeing your face is pretty scary,

But your Mom is downright eerie.

I suddenly remembered the song the kids at
school chanted at me and cringed. Then, staring at my
shaking fingers, I saw another strange occurrence: my
nails had grown extra-long. What was happening?
Looking into the fluorescent light caused an unbearable
burning in my eyes, making it almost impossible to see
my reflection in the mirror. The most difficult part of
the procedure was brushing my hair. My hair seemed to
have increased in length and fullness overnight.

The possibility that my appearance might be changing

was just one more horrifying realization I couldn't accept or fathom. Tears welled up in my eyes. My whole life was being chipped away piece by piece! Everything that had been mine was being taken away by something I couldn't even understand as yet. It was an elusive, thieving intruder, this porphyria. More than any other emotion I had felt in the past, anger was the strongest within me, growing stronger with each defeat! That anger got me through what ended up to be an hour of concentrated attempt to look somewhat presentable.

Next, I inched my way back to the couch, grateful to lie down. I still was there when my brother and his children arrived. Trying to act normal and healthy was such a chore I could hardly manage it. How had my mother done it all these years? I sat up slowly, knowing if I moved too quickly the dizziness would knock me right down again. A headache was coming on and that was the last thing I needed. A tingling sensation had begun in both my legs, resembling the sensation I'd encountered during the lumbar procedure, but now it was more like an electrical buzzing.

Meanwhile I tried to think positively; after all, my brother, whom I loved dearly, was coming to see me. Dan and I had always had an extraordinary brother-sister relationship. We never fought as children often do. We always supported each other. I knew from Dan's eyes he was shocked seeing me this way. But as he always had, no matter what the situation, he joked lovingly with me.

"Well now, would ya look at this! All dolled up and lying on the couch like it was some sort of holiday or something!" He always had a special way of making the most gruesome of situations a little easier to handle.

The rest of the afternoon we spent talking of the past

days' events. I liked having Dan and the children's company, but it made me tired. For some reason, I didn't care. My children fussed over their three-month-old cousin, Caroline, bringing out little toys and chattering at her, trying to coax a smile. Dan offered her to me to hold and it nearly broke my heart to have to refuse. I had been so happy seeing his life unfolding so perfectly, with his new wife and new baby girl. I knew he wanted me to share a precious piece of this with him. Still, I could not trust my weak and trembling arms to hold such a special prize. I could sense their concern and frustration not being able to do anything about it. It was especially evident when I walked across the room, my right leg dragging behind me despite my effort to walk normally. Pity and sympathy were too difficult for me to handle along with everything else. The anger was there, but frustration and shame were stronger this time. I sat back down on the sofa and didn't try to get back up again until after they left.

Then Tim helped me back into bed and looked after the family the rest of the evening. He was concerned I hadn't eaten anything, but I assured him that was the last thing I wanted to do. My stomach would only reject the food. "The only thing I want is to be well! I just want to wake up in the morning and be normal for once!" More and more I was gaining sympathy for my mother despite her secretiveness.

For the next several days I was unable to get out of bed. My thoughts traveled back to the dark past. I began to see, knowing what I had learned, why Mom had hidden in the back bedroom during the "bad days." Not only had she not wanted us to see her that way but, probably, if she felt as I did, she was too weak to move.

The throbbing in my head along with the numbness in

my legs kept me prisoner. Every time I tried to lift my head off the pillow the room began to spin. The morning sunlight streaming through the window burned my eyes. What was wrong with them? Was it ever going to change? Was I always going to be like this?

We were all afraid, each of us dealing with our fear in our own separate ways. Johanna came and sat on the floor beside the bed quietly watching a movie on television. We didn't talk. I could see she just wanted to be near her mom. Reuben kept himself busy drawing pictures for me, depositing them on the nightstand on an hourly basis. Perhaps, in his innocence, he believed that his gifts would heal me. At least, he was hoping they would. Lori updated me on what was going on downstairs, letting me know she had everything under control. She had always been the strong one, feeling like it was her responsibility to keep the ship afloat. Dan? He just poked his head in the door from time to time to make sure I hadn't gone anywhere. Dan kept his thoughts and feelings to himself, as he had always done. Sometimes he was hard to read because of this. Still, I could feel his love and concern for me. The children were getting through this fearful time the best way they knew how.

I fell into an exhausted sleep. When I awoke the bedroom was dark, the house quiet. I made a cursory assessment of my condition before trying to move. It was frightening not knowing what would occur from moment to moment, or what new symptom would seize my body without warning. The headache was no longer an unbearable pounding, but had become a dull sensation of pressure. My extremities still felt as though I was hooked up to an electrical outlet. But, could it be? I was hungry for the first time in nearly two weeks!

The red glow of the alarm clock told me it was nearly eleven o'clock. My mom once told me, "It takes a lot of courage to try, and you can never truly fail if you have truly tried." It was evident that courage would have to become one of my strongest qualities. Courage would walk me down the stairs and prepare my food. Courage would replace fear.

Holding onto furniture, steadying myself against the wall, I maneuvered the stairs in a record-breaking three minutes! A little victory! Turning the corner into the dining room, a strange sensation, a new one, overwhelmed me. It was as if someone hooked a garden hose to an opening at the top of my head and turned it on full blast! The rushing water gushed through every part of my body at a high rate of speed. My hands shook uncontrollably; goose bumps appeared on my upper arms; tiny hairs on my back I'd never known before tickled my skin. And then the sensation left as mysteriously as it appeared. My medical condition, porphyria or whatever it was, had become a terrifying and mystifying chain of events.

My wonderful husband stood in the kitchen, greeting me with a dish towel in his hand. He was so strong for me and the children.

"I feel really guilty about this. I keep thinking I could have done something to prevent it," I said to him.

"You are such a silly girl." He smiled at me, wrapping his arms around my shoulders. "None of this is your fault. How could you have done anything about it?"

"I don't know. Maybe if I had gone to the doctor more often or demanded more tests. I just feel like I should have taken more control over my health."

"Well," he said, "you're not a doctor. And, even if you were, you probably wouldn't have caught on to what was happening."

"You're right. I guess the only thing we can do is wait for the test results and go from there," I said. "Until then, I'll just concentrate on getting better. Speaking of which, I am feeling kind of hungry."

"Are you serious?"

"Yes, I'm serious! Is there anything left, or did the kids scarf it all?"

Tim began frantically searching through each cupboard. "You just sit right there," he said. "I'll find something for you. What sounds good? Cereal? Pasta? A sandwich?"

"How about that pie over there on the bar? That looks pretty good. Who made it?"

"Lori did. It's cherry, your favorite. She wanted to bake one just for you."

"Well, I'd better have a piece then," I teased. "I wouldn't want to disappoint her."

Slicing Lori's homemade cherry pie and pouring a glass of juice, Tim brought them to me. "I'm so happy you're going to eat this," he said. "You'll never know how happy."

He sat down beside me. "We've been through bad times before, my love. The good Lord has always seen us through them, and He will this time, too. You'll just have to take it slowly." Tim's voice held strength and love.

I wanted to believe him. I wanted so desperately to believe that this too would pass!

I tried to carry Tim's optimism with me as I crept back to bed. However, within minutes the pressure on my spine was more intense than ever! It felt strangely numb in that spot. Now it was in the lower part of my back as well. I had noticed walking to the bedroom my balance was off again, too. The tremors were getting worse, especially in my legs. I told myself Tim was right about taking it slow. I tried not to feel disappointed.

Later that week, I decided to venture outdoors. I wanted so badly to breathe fresh air and to see our garden. But, as I walked to the window and opened it just to look out, the morning sunlight scorched my eyes. I had the feeling that the sun had now become a lifelong enemy. I could not stop my tears.

"Not doing too well today?" Tim walked into the room and tried to comfort me.

I didn't answer. I tried to stop crying. Somehow it seemed easier just to turn away from him and try to keep all the hurt and frustration to myself.

"How about some lunch? It's all ready. All you have to do is come downstairs. Or, if you want, I can fix you a tray and bring it up to you. Whatever you want."

"Thanks, but I'm not hungry."

"Well, maybe just some coffee then. I'll bring some up."

"Can't you understand?" I yelled at him. The tears flooded back, bringing with them all the stored-up emotions from within me. "I can't eat, or drink, or even look outside! I can't feel the things that I touch, or even walk down the stairs without falling down! Or pick up things without their breaking! I can't do anything anymore! Oh God! Why don't you just let me die?"

Tim held me in his arms as I cried, wiping each tear away from my face as it fell. "Shh. There now. There."

"I'm sorry, I know it's not right to feel this way, but I can't help it. I just want to be normal again! How could you possibly love me the way I am now!"

"You are my heart, Tammy. You are my whole life," he said. "I will always love you no matter what. I made a promise, remember?"

Despite his words, I was losing my will to survive and taking all that Tim held dear with me. In many ways he was suffering much more than I was. I tried to regain my composure.

"Would you like some good news?"

I knew he was attempting to change the subject, to give me some hope for the future. What could be good?

"Dr. Stewart's office called this morning," Tim said.

"What?"

"Remember? The doctor at the clinic your mother's seeing. He has the results from the porphyria test. I made an appointment for us to see him tomorrow morning."

"Why would *he* have the results? I thought Dr. Ratliff ordered the tests," I objected.

"Apparently he turned your case over to Dr. Stewart. I guess he's the one who will be handling it now."

"Well, did he say what the results were? Do I have porphyria?"

"Actually, I didn't talk to him. His secretary is the one who called. Maybe the news will be the respite we've all been waiting for," Tim said hopefully.

"Or maybe it's more bad news," I said pensively.

"Tammy, let's think positively. There's no sense worrying about it any more." Tim smiled a wan smile. "Now, how about that coffee?"

I shook my head. I knew Tim was right: there was no use speculating. Dr. Stewart's office had called, perhaps he had the key to unlock this mystery. Fear held me firmly in its grip.

Chapter 10

Facing the Enemy

It was my first time out of the house since I'd come home from the hospital. Before we left, Tim found an old pair of clip-on sunglasses to put on my prescription glasses so the sunlight wouldn't hurt my eyes. That did help somewhat, but the process of making it from the house to the car was so strenuous that I didn't even take the time to enjoy the outdoors I had so wanted to see.

The first part of the drive to Petoskey was uneventful. During the final hour we had to pick our way through a blinding snowstorm. I kept telling myself not to think of it as an omen.

Dr. Stewart was not at all what I had expected. Instead of the gray-haired, serious "looks like he's been locked in a research lab for twenty years" kind of guy, he seemed to be kind of childlike in manner. He talked fast and never seemed to stop moving. Dr. Stewart reminded me of my brother when he was a teenager, animated and spunky.

He put me through the same contortionist routine that

Dr. Ratliff had, moving me this way and that, and then sent me to the laboratory for more blood work. The lab work took a short time and then we sat in the reception room waiting to be called back in to see him. An hour passed. When we were finally allowed into his office, Dr. Stewart looked at me with a kind of odd excitement.

"Okay, Tammy. It's all right if I call you Tammy, isn't it?"

"Sure," I said. "It's all right with me."

"Good. Sorry it took me so long to get back to you. I've been on the phone with one of my colleagues at the Mayo Clinic who is a porphyria specialist. We went over your test results and have both arrived at the same conclusion."

"And what might that be?" I said, my voice trembling.

"Judging from the level of porphyrins in your blood, and the family history, I think it's safe to say that you definitely have hereditary coproporphyria." He almost looked like he was smiling.

"What?" I said, my throat hoarse. I looked over at Tim. We were both shaken.

"Oh, I'm sorry. That's just a fancy way of saying that you have a certain type of porphyria, HCP for short."

Well, there it was. After all of the suffering, doctors, and testing, we finally had a name for what was wrong with me. It was the same disease my mother had. I leaned forward in my chair. "Dr. Stewart, what do I have to do to feel better again? Is there some sort of medication I have to be on the rest of my life or a certain treatment to go through?"

He looked puzzled and sad. "Tammy, I thought you knew."

"What do you mean? Knew what?"

Suddenly the conversation was about to take on a whole new direction.

"The prognosis. You do know your mother's?"

"I thought until a short while ago she had multiple sclerosis," I told him.

His expression turned somber. He looked anxious, as if he wanted to jump up and run out of the room. Instead, he reached for my hand as if I were a child. "There is no medication to take. As of today there is no known cure for porphyria."

My head throbbed so I could hardly understand what he was saying. "Surely there must be something I can do! There has to be a doctor out there somewhere who has the cure for this!"

"The kind of porphyria you have appears to be a genetic disorder, Tammy. You were born with the gene that causes it. The only way there can ever be a cure for porphyria is by isolating that gene and altering it somehow. That technology simply isn't available to us, yet. Perhaps someday it will be."

"Are you telling me I'm not ever going to get any better than I am right now?"

"Oh no! You'll get better from this attack. At least to a certain extent. But these attacks will happen again. You will experience more acute attacks of this disease throughout your life. Each one will probably be worse than the last. Eventually. . . ."

"I'll die. That is what you're telling me, isn't it?"

"A horrible existence like this," I said. "Oh my God!"

"There is no reason to suspect that you can't live for a long time, Tammy. Here, let me try to explain it to you the best way I know how."

Tim said, "She's very ill and upset. Please explain it slowly."

Dr. Stewart went on. "Porphyria is a general term, used to describe several different types of enzyme-deficiency disorders. They all have one thing in common, an overproduction of something called porphyrins. Your body is basically poisoning itself because you lack the particular enzyme that would remove the poisons naturally. These poisons build up inside of you, gathering in indiscriminate locations and attacking your central nervous system at will. Do you understand so far?"

I nodded.

He continued. "You are very fortunate to even obtain a diagnosis of porphyria."

Somehow I didn't feel all that blessed.

"Porphyria is so highly symptomatic that it is often diagnosed as other, more common ailments, because doctors have never seen a case. Lay people call it 'The Vampire Disease.' "

"Oh my God!" I couldn't help feeling a complete loss of hope hearing that term.

"All I can do," he said sadly, "is monitor your symptoms: the inability to stand sunlight, eye problems during the day, even personality changes." Then he mentioned one more symptom that I had not even been paying attention to, and that was tachycardia. "Your heart is racing and has been racing for an average one hundred fifty beats per minute during this attack. "This may be the most dangerous part of the disease. You'll need to learn to monitor your heart rate on a regular basis and reduce your stress."

With tears streaming down my face, I asked him,

"Are the other symptoms ever going to leave? Look at me. I'm a monster."

He shook his head. "Some will, but your symptoms will probably worsen as I said. There is no cure for porphyria and because of the recurring tachycardia you aren't eligible for the one symptom-suppressing treatment that is available. And there is the possibility, which I have to tell you, of invalidism or death."

At that point, I thought, looking at him, he looked like he felt like crying, too. He made it clear that when a porphyria attack had neurological effects to this magnitude there was little the body could do to repair itself. "The only hope you have of living a somewhat normal life is to avoid the attacks." He looked away as he went on. "There is not much more that can be done, at least not at this time. It is frustrating to both of us that we cannot heal your body. The only literature I've been able to come up with is a small excerpt from a medical encyclopedia I read at home," he said. "For now," he added, "there are just a few basic rules to follow. The 'don'ts' include avoiding alcohol, all medications including over-the-counter meds, stress, and sunlight. There is only one 'do.' Ingest large amounts of simple carbohydrates, especially at the onset of an attack.

"As for the rest," Dr. Stewart said, "you're basically on your own. Over time you'll learn the best way to handle your porphyria attacks." At this point he paused and then said, "It probably would be helpful for you to make the trip to Minnesota to be examined by the specialist, if for no other reason than to add your case history to his research."

As we were leaving, Dr. Stewart handed us five large plastic containers for urine collection. "All four of your

children need to be tested, along with your brother. I'll
have the results of their tests on your next visit to me."

I had not even considered that my children might be
afflicted as well. My heart contracted at the thought that my
children would ever be this ill. *No, God! No! You cannot
have my babies. Take me, but let my babies live!*

Dazed and confused, Tim and I left the hospital. We
now knew the name of the dreaded ailment—PORPHYRIA!
"The Vampire Disease." That wasn't much comfort.

At the desk the secretary smiled as she handed Tim a
piece of paper. "Here you go, Mr. Evans. These are the
instructions for your children. Just make sure you follow them
exactly and have the bottles back here as soon as you can."

Chapter 11

A Homecoming of Sorts

We drove back home, through another snowstorm like the one we encountered on the way there. The darkness outside echoed our mood.

"What are we going to do?" I asked Tim.

"I don't know," he answered. He sounded distant, separated from me somehow.

"The children have had so much to deal with already. It's difficult enough for you and me to understand all the new things we've learned about this disease today. And now we've got to find a way to tell them the horrible news...that they could have it, too! It keeps getting worse and worse. God...how am I gonna protect my children from the curse? How am I gonna tell them?"

"I told you, I just don't know!" Tim stomped on the brakes and, though we both had on seat belts, the force drove us forward from our seats. The van skidded to a stop on the side of the road. He jumped out, slamming the door hard behind him. Tim was as angry and frustrated as I was. For weeks he had been so positive, so strong, keeping our family going, guarding the children from the knowledge of the awful pain that wracked my body. Up to this point, there didn't seem like there could be anything so awful that it would diminish his strength and fortitude. However, the fact that the children might be plagued by this horrible nightmare was just too much for him. Like me, he could not bear to consider that they would fall prey to this vicious disease. Like my mother, he just wanted to pretend the disease would go away, in order to deny to himself the possibility his children would be afflicted.

From the window I watched the snow landing in clumps on his back. Tim was slumped over the hood of the idling van. His arms were wrapped tightly around his head in grief, hiding his tears from me. I was taken aback, helpless, seeing him surrender to the pain that he had for so long kept locked up inside.

He wept uncontrollably like a frightened child unsure of the future. I got out and went to him, wrapping my arms securely around his snow-covered body.

"I'm sorry. I don't know what came over me," he said hoarsely.

"Hey, you don't have anything to be sorry about. It's been a very rough day," I whispered, trying to console him.

His fist slammed against the wet hood of the van. "This just isn't fair! We're good people, you and me. I don't understand. Why is this happening to us?"

"I can't answer that either," I said, wiping the falling snow from his face. "Maybe it's some kind of test."

"Well," he sighed, turning his head up towards the darkened sky. "You can quit anytime now, God! I don't think

I can handle any more."

"I don't think it works that way, hon. We can't second-guess the reason for all this. We'll just have to accept it and try to deal with it the best way we can. Together."

Tim looked into my eyes. "I could never make it without you, you know that."

I forced a smile. "I told you before, I'm not going anywhere. We're going to fight this thing together. You, me, the kids, we're a team," I reassured him. "C'mon, it's getting colder and you're soaked to the bone. The last thing we need is for you to get sick."

"I love you," he said as we got back into the car. His eyes searched for a promise, a guarantee that I would remain with him. He knew I didn't have the power to make such a pledge. However, at that moment it didn't matter. My words alone would give him the strength he needed to face the children.

"I will love you . . . forever."

The night passed and morning followed. I was still locked in a dreamless sleep. The knock at the bedroom door startled me! The trip to Petoskey had tired me more than I had expected it would. Perhaps this new fatigue was of the spirit as well as the body.

"Momma?"

I heard a familiar voice from behind the door.

"Is that you, Reuben?"

"Is it all right if I come in?" The door slowly opened, and he peeked around it. Seeing my son's baby face immediately warmed my heart and spirit, although he hated my commenting on the fact that his face still had a baby's soft-skinned smudge of a nose. The twinkle in his deep blue eyes was always a welcome and comforting sight to me.

"I'm not really supposed to be up here, Momma," he whispered. "Dad said we had to give you time to get better and to let you sleep." He tiptoed over to the side of the bed, kneeling down at my side.

"So, where is Dad right now, buddy?" I stroked the soft golden strands of his feathery hair.

"He's on his way back to Petoskey to take the pee containers back. We're all done with the peepee now."

I couldn't help laughing at the way he described the specimens. "I bet you're glad that's over."

"It wasn't so bad. Kind of like camping, in a way," he said, nestling his head in the crook of my arm. "How long before we'll know if we have porphyria, Momma?"

His innocent questioning stabbed deeply into my already breaking heart. There was no way to tell for certain when the test results would come in. The samples from each of the children had to be sent to the Mayo Clinic laboratory in Minnesota. The clinic in Petoskey didn't have the facilities or the expertise to diagnose such a rare condition. "We won't know anything until my next appointment with Dr. Stewart and that's in two weeks."

I didn't want Reuben to become more anxious; so I changed the subject. "Why don't you come up here and snuggle with me for a while," I said to my son. He still liked to cuddle up to his mother. It created a safe space for both of us, making us feel close to each other.

"Are you sure? It won't hurt you or anything, will it?"

"No, not at all. It will probably make me feel better. I've been missing you guys a lot."

"I've been missing you, too, Momma." He crawled in under the covers, trying to be careful not to jostle my body around too much. It felt so good to have him next to me.

"Reuben, are you worried about how your tests will turn out?"

"No." He paused. "Not really. I'm not sick like you are, so I probably don't have it. I just want you to feel better. You *are* going to get better soon, right?"

"Well, the doctor said I would get stronger if I rest and take care of myself. And, you know, I believe I am feeling better than I was yesterday, so it must be working." I could feel him rustling around under the comforter, like he was looking for something. His hand appeared from under it, holding a small, oval-shaped butterscotch disk wrapped in yellow cellophane.

"Here. I got this for you today. Dad told us that you have to eat a lot of candy to get better. I hope it's okay that I spent my allowance on sweets this time. I know you usually don't like it when I do that."

"It's fine, son," I said with tears in my eyes.

Once again, as he had done so many times in the past, Reuben had found a way to melt my heart. He had put his own fear aside, the fear that he could have this terrible sickness that he had been witnessing in me. Putting those he loved first came very easily to him. If Mom needed candy to get better, then he would get it. How could I complicate the childhood simplicity by revealing the complexities of my illness? Only the peaceful serenity of this unselfish gesture, and my acceptance of it, was of any significance in that special moment between us.

"Oh, thank you, son. Look!" I said, unwrapping the

piece of candy from the cellophane covering, "I'll eat it right now."

"Don't you worry, Momma. I bought a whole bag of them. Whenever you need one, just let me know and I'll get it for you." His eyes sparkled with delight as he watched me pop the candy into my mouth. He leaned over close to my ear whispering, "I hid the bag under my mattress so the other kids won't take any. It'll be our little secret."

"That's a good idea," I whispered back. "I won't tell if you won't."

He winked at me with a sheepish grin. "That's a deal, Momma."

"Well, buddy, I think I'm feeling a little better after the sweets, so I'll come downstairs for a while and see how everybody's doing."

"That'll be great!"

Reuben jumped out of the bed and came around to my side to offer me his arm. "Lean on me so you don't fall."

We walked down the stairs together. Reuben set the pace, cautiously guarding each step I took. I could see that it made him feel important to be helping me this way. Just as I settled into the chair at the kitchen table, the phone rang. Reuben raced over and grabbed it so I wouldn't have to get up again.

"It's Uncle Dan," he said, handing me the receiver.

"Hello?"

"Hey, it's good to hear your voice. How are you feeling?" my brother asked.

"Pretty good, I think. I just got up a few minutes ago."

"Tammy, Tim said you weren't doing too well after the doctor's appointment. He called about the sample they wanted me to give for testing."

"So, did you?"

I wasn't sure if he would. Dan never did face illness well, especially when it involved himself. He liked to see himself as strong, completely impervious to any kind of physical impairment.

"I finished the test this morning and it's all ready to go, but I don't know where to take it." Knowing Dan, I was sure he didn't plan on getting the sample in.

"Tim just left a little while ago to take the kids' samples back to Petoskey. I guess you'll have to take yours back there, too."

"I'm too busy to be fiddling around with this kind of thing. Chelene will have to drive the sample up there tomorrow if she has time. If not, I guess I just won't be tested."

"Dan, you can't just pass this off like it's not important. We're talking about your life."

"I feel just fine! I don't see why I had to do this in the first place. I'm not sick!" He sounded agitated, like this whole thing was nothing but an inconvenience in his busy schedule.

"Just listen to me a minute, Dan. I've been reading the information Dr. Stewart gave me. It says you could have porphyria and not even know it. Not everyone is symptomatic. Women show early signs of the disease. Men don't. Some people don't show signs of having it until they're elderly. And we know now Mom and her father had it."

"Sure. I know that it runs in the family. That's all I need to know!" he snapped back.

"Fine! If you want to stick your head in the sand, then go right ahead! But, before you do, you'd better start thinking about Caroline!"

I had struck a sore spot. Like me, he hadn't thought
about the fact that his child could have porphyria. Dan didn't
respond for several seconds. When he finally did, it was the
somber pouting of having been rebuked. "You're right. I didn't
think of it that way. I'll make sure Chelene takes the container back in the morning."

"Good."

"Tammy, if it turns out that I have it, what exactly can
be done to make sure I never get sick?"

It was a fair question, one that I had asked Dr. Stewart.
Unfortunately, neither he nor I had the answer. "I don't know,
Dan. I'm not sure anything can be done. Maybe the specialist
at the Mayo Clinic will be able to help. Let's just deal with
one thing at a time. I have to see Dr. Stewart again in two
weeks. He should have all the results back by that time. Until
then, we'll just have to wait."

"I gotta go. You take care of yourself, you hear?"

I could tell he didn't want to talk about the subject any
longer.

"I will. And don't worry."

I was telling my little brother to do something I myself
was not capable of doing. Of course he was going to worry!
We all were. Until we knew for sure how many of us were
affected and what options were available to us, there was
nothing to do *but* worry. Still, I tried to sound convincing...
for his sake.

"Call me back when you hear anything. Talk to you
later."

"Goodbye, Dan. I love you."

"Love you, too."

We made it through another night. The next morning

as the children left for school they informed me that, though Dad had tried, if I didn't go shopping soon we were all going to starve to death! The only food in the house was a casserole which my mother had brought. It dawned on me it had probably been three weeks since any major grocery shopping had been done. Fortunately, Tim didn't have a busy day scheduled. We would have to go when he came home. There was no way I could shop on my own.

Next, I called the manager at the store where I hoped I still had employment. He was very kind, reassuring me that my job was waiting for me. He said they could work out a reduced schedule or whatever I needed. We discussed the fact that I wouldn't be able to work until receiving the green light from the doctor and that wouldn't be for, at least, another month.

"It's not a problem, Tammy, and everyone wants you to know they miss you. You've been our best security officer and I'd hate to lose you."

That gave me some hope. I missed working. Although we didn't really need the extra income, the money was nice. Since the kids were gone all day at school, it had become an escape from an empty home more than anything else. Knowing it was going to be quite a while before I could go back was hard for me to accept.

When Tim arrived home I made sure I had my "shades" on, and I wore a sloppy sweatsuit and scarf to cover as much of my skin as possible. Of course, my swollen, blotched face still showed. I convinced Tim that letting me shop would help me feel useful and so he agreed to take me. In the grocery store I held onto the grocery cart so I wouldn't lose my balance. Tim put the food in the cart as we rolled up and down the aisles ever so slowly. Every few minutes we saw another shopper stop to stare at me. I tried to ignore them. It was obvious by the look on each one's face that I looked freakish. Despite wanting to get it all over with quickly, it took two hours to finish the food-gathering. When it was over and we were home, I was whipped and even more dispirited. I slept hard for hours. When I woke, pain bounced around my body like little silver balls inside a pinball machine.

Somehow I crept downstairs, where Mom and Dad waited. I couldn't seem to accomplish the smallest task like lifting a cup of coffee without it smashing to the floor or brushing my hair without having to stop every few strokes to rest my arm. It was very discouraging. Trying to raise my spirits, Dad said he had seen it take months for Mom to be able to perform those simple tasks after an attack. He didn't tell me, but I found out later some symptoms never returned. Dad encouraged me to keep trying and to never give up. He had brought over a supply of vitamins including vitamin B and beta keratin. Mom had a shorter recovery when taking those two particular vitamins together. Maybe. At that point, anything was worth a try.

After the years of not knowing, I was finally able to relate to what my mother had gone through. Remembering the time that she had hidden her porphyria from my brother and me, I was now able to feel what she felt. It was not just the embarrassment of our family seeing her in a weakened condition that had made her withhold the truth. More than that, it was fear. The fear of not knowing if she would live through each attack, or die before she had an opportunity to recover. I felt it now. When the pain became so bad that I felt

I could not take another breath, when the dry heaves lasted for hours on end, those were the times that it seemed it would be much easier to just hide myself away and die.

The thought of death was both friend and enemy at the same time. As a friend, death invited you to a place where there was no more agony, a place so wonderful that you forgot you even had pain and suffering. As an enemy, it ripped you away from those who loved you, leaving them to grieve at your absence. I saw my mother's flirtation with death clearly now. At times throughout her life, when the attacks were at their worst, she must have beckoned death, welcoming it with outstretched arms. It was those times she must have considered it a friend. No, I told myself, my place is here, with Tim and my children, and for them. They would need me here to explain it all. And if, God forbid, the children had the disease, they would need me to help them find out how to stop the porphyria from causing so much pain.

All we could do now was wait for the children's verdict, and waiting was proving to be the most difficult part of all. I prayed the only prayer I could:

"You have promised, Lord, that you will never give me more than I can handle. I do not have as much confidence in my ability as You seem to. My strength is failing, but I'll try to carry this burden if I have to. But, please, please, God, hear the prayer of a mother and spare my precious babies! Do not allow my children to suffer this dreadful affliction."

Chapter 12

Searching for Answers

Tim and I were ushered into Dr. Stewart's office. The past two weeks had been torturous. All kinds of frightening scenarios raced through my mind each time I looked at one of my children. Not knowing was definitely the worst part of it. I wanted to be able to reassure them that everything would be all right, as I had done with all of the other bad things that had come into their young lives. This time I couldn't, and they knew it.

I sat down, fidgeting nervously in the chair, leafing through pages of the old magazine I picked up. Tim paced back and forth, his shoes squeaking on the tile floor each time he took a step. Every few minutes he looked at me expectantly. But neither the doctor nor the nurse appeared. An hour passed. What could possible be keeping him?

"Sorry, folks!" Dr. Stewart burst through the door, catching us unaware. "Doesn't seem to be enough hours in the day anymore. So, tell me, how are you?"

"I'm feeling better, actually," I said wistfully. "Really."

"Let's just take a look," he reached for my wrist.

"Your pulse is better," Dr. Stewart said, watching me intently.

"Now," he said, picking up a large manila folder. "Let's go over the test results."

My heart pounded. Tim and I held tightly to each other's hands, waiting silently for the final verdict.

"Dr. Winston and I conferred on the results just a short time ago, Tammy. I wanted to be absolutely sure before I discussed this with you today." He flipped through each of the five pages of test results. And then he said, "All of the porphyrins in your children were in the normal range."

I breathed a sigh of relief. "Thank you, God!" Tim and I said simultaneously.

"I want to give you a word of caution." Dr. Stewart put the folder on his desk, and his voice deepened. "What this means is that your children are not showing signs of the disease at this time. It does not mean that they don't have the gene that causes porphyria."

He explained that it only meant that they were not symptomatic at that time. Most people who test positive for porphyria are tested during an attack, when there are more porphyrins in their systems. And, most porphyriacs do not become symptomatic until sometime after puberty. The tests only revealed that the porphyrin count was not elevated enough to diagnose the children as having the disease. We would need to have them tested again later in life or if they began showing signs of having porphyria. Again, it would be left up to me to decide what were symptoms and what were not.

I was confused. I had been under the impression that

he was testing the children to see if they had porphyria. "What kind of testing do they have to go through to see if they have that particular gene?" I asked.

He shook his head. "There is no test for that, not right now anyway. Relatively speaking, isolating genes is a new concept in the medical world. And, although there is tremendous progress in this new area, I'm afraid it will be a long time before porphyria will be investigated. As you know, there are many different variations of the disease so untold numbers of people could be suffering without a proper diagnosis."

"I don't understand," I told him. "Does that mean you'll have to monitor the children somehow to make sure they never become sick?"

"No, Tammy. I am not the one who will monitor them. That's going to be your job."

"*My job!* I wouldn't know what to look for! How could I possibly look for signs of something which I don't understand?"

"There are probably a lot of things that happened to you along the way that were diagnosed as other ailments that were, in reality, symptoms of your disease. Moreover, I think if you look back on all that has taken place with your health over the years, you will see a progression in your illness."

His suggestion was curious. With all the other things to be concerned about I hadn't yet considered the possibility that many of my illnesses were attacks of this disease.

"It would be a good idea for you to start a journal and put down your medical history," he said. "Go back over all the times you've been ill and try to ascertain whether there is any correlation between those events and porphyria."

"I see what you're getting at, Dr. Stewart. But how would it help the children?" I asked.

"Tammy, I have to level with you. Physicians don't know a lot about the numerous symptoms of porphyria. New ones that we've never seen before crop up in patients all the time, and we are just beginning to find out there are different types of the disease. Right now, I would have to say that you know as much about the intricacies of this disorder as anyone else."

How could he possibly think such a thing! I had just found out I had the disease, and now I'd been qualified as an expert! If I knew a lot, what did that say about the others, especially doctors who were expected to know about diseases? It was an overwhelming task he was demanding that I undertake. Not only would I have to be responsible to handle my own porphyria, but I would also have to look for signs of the disease in my children.

"Dr. Stewart, I've read the material you've given me, and I've tried to understand it. But it's in medical jargon, and it's only a few pages. Isn't there more information? Can't you give me a more detailed and easier to understand guide?"

"I'm really very sorry, Tammy. But there just isn't anything else. There isn't a support group I can recommend, or a special hotline to call. Porphyria is just unknown. In truth, you only have yourself and your own experiences to rely on. To help your children you'll have to search inside yourself for the answers."

It sounded like he was offering me a sphinx-like puzzle which medical experts pondered, but did not understand and expecting me, who knew nothing of medicine, to solve it. How could he expect that? What did this puzzle have to do with helping my family get their lives back? I sighed and clutched Tim's hand. My own were trembling.

"What about my brother's results, Dr. Stewart? Are they negative as well?"

He shook his head. "I'm afraid not. Although he has never been symptomatic, Dan's porphyrin level is quite high. Dr. Winston and I have concluded that he has the disease, too."

It was the answer I had been dreading. "I see," I said, although in truth I didn't see anything.

Dr. Stewart looked at his watch, signaling that he was in a hurry once again. "Although I'm going to discuss this disease with him, perhaps it would be better coming from you first. When you tell him about the porphyria, make sure you let him know that he should go with you to the Mayo Clinic. Dr. Winston will want to gather all the research he can on your family history. I'll have the test results sent to your brother, but I think it would be much better if he heard the news from you first."

Dr. Stewart hopped up from his chair, checking his watch again. "I really do have to get going," he said.

I still had more questions, but his hurried demeanor made it difficult for me to think. I called to him as he turned to go out the door. "Please, doctor, there's something I really need to know about my own case. My legs and arms! I have to know. Is the paralysis ever going to go away?"

The compassion I had seen in his eyes once before returned briefly. "I wish I could say yes, but I just don't know. You may never recover any more than this, Tammy, or you may. . . . We'll just have to wait and see."

He waved a cursory goodbye to us before leaving the room. Tim and I felt abandoned by him. Standing up, we held each other close, hoping that this bonding would give us the strength to face the uncertainty of our future.

As we walked to our car we were silent. Each of us withdrew to our own thoughts. Perhaps they were unknowingly the same. The children—we would have to explain this situation to them, but how? What had, at first, seemed good news was really only an interim report. They were potentially in as much danger as ever.

As we drove home, I felt dread rising inside me. It was the first time since we'd married that I regretted having to go home. How I wished we could postpone telling the children! But the inevitable couldn't be avoided. Too soon we were there.

Walking to the house, I was surprised to discover my mother had come over and was busily preparing dinner. The children were all sitting around the kitchen table quietly doing their homework. I wondered to myself what magical spell grandmothers put on their grandchildren that make them appear so angelic.

"How ya doing, kids," Tim said, trying to make his voice jovial.

"Great, Dad," they said in unison, even as their eyes, turning to look at us, were apprehensive. And I knew deep within myself that the cause of their fear was me.

Mom broke the awkward mood. "Let's all sit down to dinner. We can talk then."

The table in the dining room was covered by our lace cloth. As we walked over, Tim and I clasped each of the children's hands. I waited until everyone sat down.

"I know you've all been waiting. . . ." I felt my heart beating wildly in my chest and took a deep breath. "Well, there is some good news. As of now, none of you have porphyria."

The kids yelped with joy and gave each other pats on the back. I hated to risk destroying their good spirits.

"But," I said slowly, "porphyria is located in the genes and the tests they have can't tell if you might get it someday."

"Someday all of us may get it?" Lori asked, looking around at her siblings.

I nodded. "After puberty, as I did."

"But maybe we won't," Reuben said.

I loved his optimism.

"That's what we'll be praying for," Mom said.

Though Tim attempted to make conversation, we finished Mom's delicious chicken and mashed potatoes in silence.

It wasn't until we all got up to clear the dishes that I noticed my mother limping on her left leg and her hands trembling. "Mom, are you having an attack?" I asked.

She finally admitted she had been ill for several days. "But I didn't want to say anything because you all have enough to deal with."

Tears rose to my eyes as I realized the effort she had made to be there and cook our dinner.

"I feel terrible," I said, but she broke in.

"Tammy, I did it because I love you and I know how difficult this is—to bear not only your own illness, but the possibility the children may have it. In that way it was easier for me. Until recently doctors didn't know what this damned illness was and the thought that it could be passed on wasn't even considered. I'm so sorry, Tammy."

"I only wish I could help you, Mom."

She looked at me dragging my right arm and leg and suddenly burst out laughing. Tim and I, realizing the absurdity of my offer, joined her.

"Oh, right! You're going to help me? Okay, Tam," Mom chortled. "Here's what we'll do. Since your right side is gone and my left side is gone, we'll lock arms and drag our bum sides around between us!"

As the children joined the laughter, just for fun Mom and I tried it. We joked about ourselves the rest of the evening and it felt so refreshing to add some levity to the situation.

We were having such a good time, I was almost able to ignore the runaway pain which had settled in my right leg and right arm for the night. Tomorrow it would probably be some place else. Mom, Tim, the children and I agreed that, since there was nothing that could be done to help us, we might as well laugh at having porphyria. We all still had our senses of humor and, as far as we knew, there wasn't anyway the disease could take that away from us, if we didn't allow it to.

Chapter 13

More Chaos

Our lives were beginning to resemble a runaway train ride that we were desperate to get off and yet unable to find a way. Although my body tired easily, I could be active for an hour or two at a time, but then I felt exhausted. The pain in my right arm was constant. There was weakness in that arm, too. Lifting even medium-sized containers of milk took all my strength. Walking, however, was becoming easier now with the exception of going up and down stairs. I fell down the basement stairs one day and didn't tell Tim because he wouldn't have let me stay home alone again. Besides, it wasn't good for my family to be continually reminded that I was weak and in pain. I wouldn't get any stronger if I didn't try to do things for myself. And if I was not strong, my family could not be strong.

Despite my efforts, I had begun noticing that my thinking process was not as clear as it used to be and that I became confused easily. The doctor had warned me that the mental confusion could be part of the symptoms, but I hadn't given it much credence at the time. However, I began forgetting simple things and that frightened me. One week I forgot to go to the drugstore to buy vitamins, then halfway back home, I remembered and went back to the drugstore only to forget why I was there. Another morning I stood in the middle of Kmart with no clue as to what I was doing there. My mental state scared and humiliated me. The feeling of defeat was overpowering. In addition, I forgot more important things like a dentist appointment for Reuben. I didn't even bother to give my legitimate excuse. It was much easier not to give the dental receptionist a two-hour dissertation on my struggle with porphyria. It was not an unreasonable hope that my memory problem would pass or at least diminish somewhat. Realistically, I knew it might worsen. Moreover, I couldn't seem to control my emotions. Sometimes, when shopping, I couldn't make it through the parking lot and into the van before some little kid yelled, "Hey, Mommy, why is that lady crying?"

Regardless of how well I hid these symptoms from my family, I was coming to the realization that I would probably not be able to return to work. There, my memory loss and physical problems could land me in real trouble. I would have to put aside my desire to work outside the home, at least for the present.

Mom was finally going to the hospital in Petoskey. The attack she began to have shortly after I returned home from seeing Dr. Stewart was now too intense to ignore. After all these years, I finally understood her stubbornness in not wanting to be hospitalized. Recently, I had thought it was cruelty to herself and to us making us all suffer her pain, but now I was able to see my mother in a different light. Her stubbornness was instigated by the tremendous fear of never coming home again, the fear of dying and the fear of leaving us all behind.

I finally wrote to the doctor at the Mayo Clinic as Dr. Stewart had suggested:

Dear Dr. Winston,

Recently, I was diagnosed with hereditary coproporphyria by Dr. Jonathan Stewart at the Wyatt Clinic. The testing was performed in your lab, and I was told that you had confirmed the results. Dr. Stewart has scheduled an appointment for me with you. However, before making such a trip, I would like to ask a few questions.

I have been informed of several measures I must take in order to avoid further attacks of this disorder (i.e., rest, eat carbohydrates, avoid alcohol and medications). Is there anything else that could be done to reduce my risk of attack or bring me any closer to being cured altogether?

Quite frankly, I cannot afford to make such an extensive trip if there is nothing you can do to help me. My medical insurance has yet to respond to the bills I have already incurred relating to my last porphyria attack. I am sure they would not cover any further examinations or tests, since I am not currently in an emergency situation. Is there a possibility that my visit could be covered by a grant to your research program? If so, I would make every effort to keep my appointment.

Thank you in advance for your reply. Also, if you have any information about porphyria, I would appreciate it.

Sincerely,

Tammy Evans

Maybe Dr. Winston knew something which would
benefit either my mother or me. Still, it felt strange asking for
help from someone I didn't even know. What I had written in
the letter was painfully true. Although money hadn't ever
been a problem since my marriage to Tim, the bills from my
hospital stay and the lab tests were pouring in like crazy. Dr.
Stewart still wouldn't allow me to go back to work. If he had,
we could have paid many of them. Deep down, I knew Tim
was right, though. It was no longer possible for me to endure
a full day of any kind of activity, no less work, without resting
every few hours. The insurance company had not sent any
notification as to whether they were intending to pay anything
on these bills or not. There were no assigned codes or pay
rates to attach to my diagnosis. Porphyria was just as much a
mystery to them as it was to me. Nevertheless, I didn't have
much to lose by asking such straightforward questions. In
fact, I didn't have anything else to lose at all.

Winter was slowly drawing to a close. During the long
months I recuperated and tried to learn as much as I could
about porphyria. Tim and I spent many hours at the library
searching through the endless rows of encyclopedias and
medical books. There was little written about the disease and
what we found was similar to the information Dr. Stewart
had given me. The information we came up with described
porphyria as a rare, life-threatening disorder with neurological
manifestations. The newer entries told about the genetic
component. We used dictionaries to look up the unfamiliar
medical terms.

"Here's something interesting." I motioned Tim over
to me. "This says that the word porphyrin is a Greek word
derived from ancient Egyptian hieroglyphics. It was

originally used to describe a rock called porphyry, which
contained purple crystals of feldspar or quartz."

"What else does it say?"

"'Porphyrins are organic pigments derived from the
breakdown of hemoglobin and chlorophyll,'" I read.

Tim thought it over for a minute. "So, if these porphyrins are what cause your body to poison itself, then we
can describe the disease as the purple poison." He grinned,
"At least that will make you colorful to the children."

After days of investigating the medical and technical
terms, we searched the library's computer for other sources of
the word porphyria. There was only one other article. It briefly
mentioned the disorder, and added some startling news.

"King George III was thought to have suffered from a
rare genetic disorder known as porphyria."

That was all it said. The words left us intrigued in a
strange sort of way. The mere mention of King George brought
me back to my high school history lessons about British
royalty. "According to them, King George was thought to
have been insane. The disease he had was referred to as the
'royal malady' and other members of British aristocracy were
thought to have suffered from it as well. Back then, anyone
who suffered from the malady, as it was called, was cast out,
hidden from the public eye. They were sent away to other
countries, so as not to betray any hint of weakness in the royal
family." I paused and looked at Tim.

"If this is true," I said, "then not much has changed in
the past two hundred years, has it?"

"What are you getting at?" Tim asked.

"After all this time, porphyria is still a fearful secret,
tucked away in the pages of history, from which onlookers

hide." He sighed and turned back to his book.

Tim and I continued our search, but our attempts to educate ourselves on the medical and technical terms gave little information, no less answers, to our questions. Dr. Stewart seemed to be right. I really do seem to know more about porphyria than anyone else. And that's an extremely discomforting revelation!

Other than the constant fatigue, I was continuing to slowly improve physically. Some days it really hurt to force my arms and legs to work properly. Other days, I could move almost normally. The stomach cramps came back from time to time but they were less intense.

My brother, Dan, had not dealt well with the news of his diagnosis. His reaction was that of denial. "I refuse to believe that this could be happening to me." I understood how he felt. It wasn't the kind of news that one easily accepted. To him it was like a bad dream which, if you ignored it, would go away. I could only hope he would never have to go through what I had been through in the past few months even though I knew that mine was an empty hope. In time, perhaps, we would be able to talk about our conditions and he would finally learn to accept the truth.

Despite Tim's and my increasing financial problems and my limited physical ability, Tim remained tenderly consistent in his support of me. His love made the unbearable bearable. "I feel helpless about my inability to nurse you back to health," he confided. Somehow though, he found the strength to face each day with a smile, a warm embrace, and a positive attitude.

One Thursday we went to the mall on a "secret mission" which usually meant we were going to the candy store for an ice cream cone. This time Tim said it was for a different purpose. Our first stop was at the jewelry store where, to my surprise, Tim asked the clerk for an item he had ordered. A moment later the young man reappeared with a small black box and handed it to Tim. When he opened it, I saw a small gold bracelet with my name inscribed on it. I turned it over to find the word POR-PHYRIA in big bold letters.

"This is for the times we can't be together," Tim said. "You need to wear this bracelet so other people will be able to help you when I can't be there." Tim spoke the words in an intimate loving whisper as he hooked the clasp around my wrist. On one hand it made me feel completely adored by this considerate, caring man. On the other hand, it made me terribly sad to have to be branded in this manner, even if it was for my own protection.

After he had given me the bracelet, Tim took me across the corridor to the store, which sold eyeglasses. He asked again for his special order and when the technician returned, she presented me with a brand new pair of gold-rimmed glasses with a special dark tint. "These are for your eyes so you can feel the warmth of the sun you always loved without pain," Tim said.

The shoppers in the mall gawked curiously as I hobbled by, wearing my new sunglasses. I knew I was a peculiar sight to them, an obviously handicapped individual, a less than perfect human specimen. Their stares held no significance for me anymore. Through the glasses and Tim's love, I had been given the ability to see the world around me without pain.

My husband refused to let this dreaded disease defeat me. He still had the strength to fight it and to keep his spirit up! I would have thought his patience and endurance would have been drained by now. It amazed me how he never failed to ask how I was feeling each morning, and how when I would repeat the same symptoms to him day after day, he would hold me in his arms, confidently stating that he knew tomorrow would be better. I yearned to possess his strength and courage, and especially his positive attitude. Maybe that was why God brought him into my life. He knew I would need Tim to encourage these things in me. Tim was my protector, my special angel. I held onto his hopes for a healthy tomorrow. But no matter how fiercely I clung to that hope, the tomorrow we both dreamed of never seemed to come.

Dear Mrs. Evans,

Please excuse my tardy response to your questions. I have been on vacation and did not receive your letter until today. It sounds like you have a good understanding of the self-management of your porphyria. Unfortunately, there is not much more I could do for you if you came to see me. The only thing I could do is repeat the same laboratory tests you have already had, and then add the information to my research. The expense of your examination and testing would be solely your responsibility, as my research is not covered by any outside grants. Thank you for your letter. Please advise my office if you intend to keep your appointment.

Best wishes,

Dr. Andrew Winston

"Well, what do we do now?" I asked, handing the letter to Tim. After all we had learned, or hadn't learned, in the previous months, Dr. Winston's response was not all that surprising. Still, it was disappointing.

"You keep writing letters until someone gives you some answers, that's what," he said. "There has to be someone out there who knows something more about porphyria."

I wrote letters, dozens of them, to physicians all over the country. I even wrote one to the First Lady at the White House, begging for her help with my situation. Out of all of them, hers was the only one to gain a reply. Her secretary wrote back, saying that my request had been forwarded to the Department of Health and Human Services. When the large manila envelope finally arrived some six weeks later, my initial excitement was immediately crushed by the contents.

The cover letter was from a Dr. Krantz, who was employed by the department. His words rebuked me for even suggesting that his agency was not concerned about porphyria and was doing nothing to educate physicians about it. He said that I had been misinformed as to the absence of research into the disorder. "I assure you, we are expending every effort to find new treatments for this rare disease."

Enclosed with the letter were pages of medical abstracts, sighting clinical research done on patients with porphyria. I read through them slowly, sorting through all of the obscure medical jargon, only to find that they didn't really say anything at all. Most of the abstracts were updated student reports of cases that were over twenty years old, describing limited histories of families much like my own. None of the information offered any real course of action or new remedies for the symptoms described. There wasn't even any mention of carbohydrate therapy or heme infusion. In essence, Dr. Krantz was doing nothing more than patting me on the head, and telling me to go away.

Nevertheless, I decided I had to try to do more, especially in regard to my children.

"Mom, have you seen my backpack anywhere?" Dan's voice had an air of frustration about it.

"Uh, I think it's down in the basement," I answered.

"Thanks, Mom. Hey, do you know where Dad keeps the mess kits by chance?"

"In my bedroom closet on the shelf."

He raced past me to the closet. Reuben was already up there, digging through the duffel bags for camping equipment. A devious smile grazed my lips as I watched the two of them scurry around in excitement. The annual Boy Scout fall camp-out was just hours away, and, as usual, they were nowhere near ready to depart.

"What are you giggling about, Madam Scouter?"

Tim came up behind me and wrapped his arms around my waist.

"Oh, nothing. It just never ceases to amaze me how they always wait until the last minute to pack." I laughed. "Isn't there something in that handbook of yours about being prepared?"

"What about you?" Tim asked. "Where's your gear?"

"Already packed and in the van, smarty pants!"

"Very good!" he said, praising me, mockingly. Tim sat down on the coffee table. His playful attitude suddenly turned serious. "Why don't you come over here for a minute. I want to talk to you about this."

"Tim, we've been over this a hundred times," I said perching myself on his lap. He was going to try again to talk me out of going on the camp-out. His work schedule had interfered with the weekend, making it impossible to fulfill his duties as assistant scoutmaster. We had decided weeks before that, if I was well enough, I could take his place. Even though I had to take precautions against the sun, I was healthy. There hadn't been any signs of the porphyria all summer long. I was in what Dr. Stewart had referred to as a type of remission.

"Now just hear me out one last time. You don't have to go if you don't want to. Mike and Sharon are both going, and I'm sure one of the other parents could take your place if we needed another adult."

"I want to go," I told him. "I really think it'll be good for me."

He shook his head in concern, knowing there was no way he was going to talk me out of it.

"I'm just worried something will happen. What are you going to do if you have an attack in the middle of the woods? There isn't a doctor within fifty miles of that place. Anyway, you've been doing too much around here."

Tim and I had decided in June to find a smaller home with all the rooms on one floor. Despite the fact that I paced myself during the moving work, there was a lot to be done in a short amount of time. We had been organizing our new home all summer. Now I wanted to go on the camping trip.

"Nothing is going to happen, so quit worrying." I unzipped the fanny pack that hung from my waist and pulled out a small plastic bag. "Look. I have my glucose tablets and candy right here. My medical card with all the information on it is here, too." I reached for his hand, drawing it to my heart. "I can't quit living, Tim. You're just going to have to let me go this time."

How I longed to be outdoors, particularly after last winter and these past months. Never had I wanted to see nature more, never had I so wanted to be a normal mother to my boys. I had come to appreciate the awesome grandeur of the great North. It was a part of me now, an essential ingredient of who I was. I could hear the crashing of the waves on the Lake Huron shore singing me to sleep each night and I would wake to gentle breezes whispering through the pines and cedars.

During the ride in our neighbors' large van, we all sang and our mood was light. In a couple of hours we were setting up camp in the heart of the Hiawatha National Forest. As I promised Tim, I let the boys do most of the work of assembling my tent and unloading the gear. Mike Bruce, the scoutmaster, and Tim had formed our troop of eight boys two years before. Sharon, Mike's wife, had also come.

We had first met briefly during the troop's planning stages. Tim and Mike had been friends for quite some time. Each of them had dropped hints to me that Sharon and I should form some sort of friendship. I didn't know anyone I could have called a close acquaintance. Ever more fearful of rejection, I had stayed to myself.

That night Sharon, Mike, and I sat around the crackling flames of the campfire, talking over the events of the day. Our boys slept soundly in their tents, giving the adults a few hours to unwind over coffee and freshly baked apple pie. Kicking off my boots, I felt more relaxed than I had in ages. Talk came naturally that night. For once I didn't feel that I had to work at seeming normal.

Sharon didn't involve herself in gossipy conversations or fruitless social hobbies. She had a serious air about her, which I found out later was an aversion to allowing too many people in her life. As we got to know each other better, I saw another side of her. Sharon had a tender heart.

"Tammy?" Sharon spoke softly.

"Yes, Sharon?"

She looked at me with an "I'm about to tell you something important" look. I leaned over to her, paying close attention to what she was about to say.

"Your boot is on fire."

Her words didn't register in my mind right away. It wasn't until I caught a whiff of melting rubber and looked down at the smoke rising up that I jumped up from my chair, grabbed my boot from under it and stomped the shoe on the ground to put out the flames. Sharon and Mike roared with laughter at my antics.

"I can't believe you guys! You sat there that whole time and let my best hiking boots catch fire!"

"Hey, Mike, look at that girl go! You were right! She really can move when there's a fire lit under her."

That was what Sharon later referred to as a test. She explained that, before she allowed people to get close to her, she would do something to test their character and ability to laugh at themselves. Not in a moral fashion, but to gain a feel for how that person responded to the bumps and bruises that are a part of life. This had definitely been a test of my fortitude. As we sat down again at the campfire, reviewing the episode, Sharon decided that I passed.

"You need to loosen up more like that, Tammy, and

not hide away. You seem like you're afraid of something, or someone. Life can be a lot more fun if you're only willing to live it."

Mike had told her bits and pieces about my illness, but he wasn't fully abreast of what it was or how seriously it affected me. Sharon and I talked long into the early morning hours about porphyria.

I scanned her face and realized she saw me no differently than other people. My physical deformities did not seem to matter. Perhaps, at last, here was the friend I'd always searched for and could confide in.

She listened intently to my every word, and asked a lot of questions. As we talked, I surprised myself by how much knowledge I had now accumulated on the subject. At the end of our conversation, she said, "I know this is the first time we've really talked, but I feel I've met a friend for life and I hope you feel the same."

I smiled.

She looked at me appraisingly. "I'm going to say what I feel."

Again I nodded.

"From what you've told me about porphyria it seems like there's only one question you haven't asked yourself." She said in deep voice leaning towards me.

"And what's that?" I said, bristling slightly.

"What are you going to do about it?" She said in a chipper voice, giving me an inquisitive look.

It was something I'd never even asked myself.

"What do you mean, what am *I* going to do about it?" Her words were a little offensive to me. *Am I again being held responsible for what happened to me?*

"Well, you said yourself there isn't much information about what to do if a person has this disease. The physicians aren't even educated enough to take care of you. There are no foundations or support groups, not even a research project to find a cure. How do you ever expect to find these answers you say you're looking for if there isn't another living soul doing anything to give them to the average person? Somebody is going to have to take on this cause, and it looks like that somebody is you. This is *your* disease, Tammy. Now, I'll say it again: What are you going to do about it?"

There it was again, the same challenge Dr. Stewart had offered me so many months ago. At that time, I didn't understand what he was trying to tell me. It wasn't until now that I recognized my growing nagging sensation for what it actually was. It was a call to action.

Tonight I had made a friend, an honest friend, one who would tell me what I needed to hear whether I liked it or not. Sharon wasn't allowing me to use suffering from porphyria as an excuse for inaction, as a way out of battling all that was wrong in the way people treat those who suffer from it. Instead, she had prodded me to use *it* as a reason for living. I began to scramble to find the way how.

A few days after the camp-out, the attack came on suddenly, just as it had done the time before. The loss of equilibrium and the excruciating pain between my shoulders came first. A couple of days later the extreme fatigue and confusion arrived. Painful stomach cramps and continual nausea were followed by open sores that blanketed my back and shoulders. My eyes couldn't stand the sunlight even through the windows. Within a week I was totally disabled.

Relentless waves of vomiting began. Tim would help me to the bathroom, waiting outside the door. The dry heaves lasted for hours at a time, completely sapping my body of all its energy. One night when he had taken me to the bathroom nearly a dozen times, he cried out, "That's it, Tammy! I just can't take it anymore! You're going to have to go to the hospital!"

"There's nothing they can do for me there, you know that." I could barely manage the words. "They'll just look at me and scratch their heads. If we do make the long trip over to Petoskey, the only thing they'll do is send me right back home!"

Tim knew I was right, but it didn't make it easier for him to handle. He had no choice but to stand over me helplessly and watch the symptoms of porphyria seize my body one by one.

On Tuesday during my second week into the attack, I felt the tachycardia. It hadn't been something all that noticeable before, but now my heart was racing as high as one hundred and fifty-four beats per minute, remaining there the rest of the night and into the next morning.

I called Dr. Stewart's office, mainly to satisfy Tim's frustration. "Nothing I've tried will stop my heart from pounding so furiously. Maybe there's something I'm missing," I said to the woman who answered the telephone.

"Unfortunately, Dr. Stewart is out of the country. I'm his office manager. I'll have to contact the doctor on call for him and he'll get back to you."

"Who is this other doctor?" I asked her.

"His name is Dr. Vandenberg, ma'am. He works with Dr. Stewart."

"Has he ever seen anyone with porphyria before?" I

was extremely hesitant because previously I had been told that no other doctor in the office handled porphyria, and I knew serious mistakes in treatment could be made.

"Oh yes, I'm sure he has," she snipped. "Being a large hospital we see many patients with it on a regular basis. Even if he hasn't handled it, I'm sure he's very familiar with it."

It was sounding like a conversation taken from the script of a Star Trek movie. It was just too weird!

"No, I think you misunderstood me. I said poor-fear-e-a."

"I heard you just fine. Like I said, it's quite common around here. It's nothing to fuss about. I'll have the doctor call you back." With that, she hung up the phone, leaving me with nothing but dead air space.

Tim could tell by my expression that I was totally astonished. When I explained to him what had just taken place, he was confused as well. It was quite obvious this lady didn't know what she was talking about and we wondered if she would even bother contacting the "doctor on call." We decided to wait for one hour. If we didn't hear anything by then, I would try to get hold of someone at the hospital in Minnesota. That idea didn't sound too appealing since we didn't know the doctors there, but it would be our only other resort. We sat at the kitchen table hoping we would hear something soon.

Dr. Vandenberg did phone back within the hour, so at least we had that much going for us. I began by telling him what the office manager had told me. He couldn't believe it. "This office sees an average of twelve thousand patients a year and out of that twelve thousand the only porphyria cases we have ever seen are you and your brother, Dan. I'm quite upset about what she said and I'm surprised she even attempted to handle the case on her own."

After that we delved into my current attack. He sounded pleasant and willing to help if he could. I explained to him that I was having an attack of tachycardia. I could hear him riffling through papers as I was talking, and I assumed he was going through my file. When I asked him what I should do, I received the most peculiar response.

"Uh, well, what would we usually do for you in this instance?"

I couldn't keep back my laughter. This was too good, I thought. Modern medicine had the technology to cure many forms of cancer, make test-tube babies, and perform transplants of major organs. Then someone like me comes along and screws everything all up, leaving hoards of doctors standing around scratching their heads.

"Well," I choked through my laughter, "excuse me for laughing, but is this role reversal here?"

He chuckled, too. "Yeah, kinda, I guess. I mean, you have to understand. The only thing I know about porphyria is what they skimmed over in medical school. They told us we would never see it and not to worry about it." He was trying to be helpful and was obviously still riffling through my file when I heard the whole stack of papers he was apparently trying to hold onto fall on the floor.

"Mrs. Evans, do you have any idea how big your file is?" He was attempting to hold the phone to his ear and pick up the papers he had dropped at the same time. "There are so many folders here, and there's one large one that contains nothing but correspondence between the doctors."

"I've never seen my file so I can't help you there."

"Don't do *anything!*"

"Just take it easy and rest. Don't overdo it."

"Ah, I see. Well, you've been very helpful."

"No, I haven't and I feel really badly that I can't do more than this," he interrupted.

"That's all right. At least I know my heart isn't going to explode."

"No, it won't explode. But, just the same, sit tight until Tuesday. I'll put your file on Dr. Stewart's desk with a note to call you right away."

"Thanks again," I said, hanging up the phone. I felt no better myself and sorry for placing him in such a predicament.

Tim listened with a blank expression as I repeated what the doctor had told me. He had no response this time, no encouraging words of hope or positive suggestions. Dejectedly, he went on getting ready to go to work. I felt so badly for him. Watching him, I felt Tim was reaching the end of his rope with me and porphyria.

After Tim left, I tottered to our bedroom with a cup of hot cocoa, pondering my circumstance. I shared Tim's anger. We were living from one acute attack to another, regrouping the best we could between each one. We were both tired of it.

Chapter 14

My Child

"Mrs. Evans?" The voice was unfamiliar to me. I could hear someone screaming in the background.

"Yes. This is Tammy Evans. May I ask who's calling?"

"This is the nurse at Alpena High School, Mrs. Evans." I could barely hear her above the screams in the background. "Your daughter Lori is in the office. She's in a lot of pain. Can you come right down and pick her up?"

"What happened?" I asked. "Did she get hurt or something?"

"I don't know exactly. Lori came running in here a few minutes ago holding her stomach. The next thing I knew she was doubled over, saying she felt like vomiting. She ran to the bathroom, when she returned she was an unearthly pale color and her body was shaking as if she were having tremors. You'd better come right away, Mrs. Evans. She seems to be in terrible pain."

A gut-wrenching pang accosted me. *Oh God*, I thought as I grabbed my pocketbook and flew out the door, not even telling Tim. *Not my daughter!* On my drive to the school a feeling of dire dread filled me. *Don't let it be this disease. Let it be a stomach flu or even appendicitis.* I drove recklessly, tears flowing from my eyes. I remembered the scene at breakfast that morning. Lori had said she couldn't finish her breakfast and passed off the irritation in her stomach as nothing more than a slight case of nausea, perhaps caused by eating her cereal too quickly. Now a few hours later, without the luxury of forewarning, the school nurse was saying her body shook with mild tremors, and icy beads of sweat glazed her clammy skin. She had said her head seemed to spin in circles. I could imagine what happened when she got to school. The glare from the fluorescent lights in the classroom must have pierced her eyes, making them burn and water. To those around her, the ones who turned to see what was happening to her, her eyes would appear as red glowing balls of fire.

By that time, it was too late. Her classmates must have noticed the metamorphosis beginning to take place. She no longer possessed the ability to conceal it from them. Lori was the kind of child who especially hated to be embarrassed. The other students, and even the teacher, must have watched with shock and curiosity as she began to turn an earthly pale color and writhe in agony as the trickery and vengeance of the poisons inside ravaged her. She must have desperately tried to hide the symptoms from them, to make her escape to the bathroom down the hall to suffer in private. Her wails of desperation would be heard echoing off the cold ceramic tiles of the lavatory walls.

I remembered my own cries at those moments: *"What is happening to me? Please, God! Make it stop!"* I could see it all. Lori hanging her head over the toilet as the nauseousness overcame her. At the same time, her bowels rumbled within, causing more pain. Nothing would actually bring relief. Both symptoms would steadily build up enormous pressure. A boiling cauldron of porphyrins was bubbling inside of her, consistently stirred by her own terror. *"Death."* I was sure that thought enticed her, taunted her. She may have even begged for it.

The vision of the episode playing out before me as I drove was too familiar. I had become intimate with its evil. As my mother before me, I had ample opportunity to become well acquainted with its tools of shame and disgrace. Its merciless howl of laughter was a voice I recognized as commonplace, nearly as powerful as the venom that ran through the veins of my family. We were alike now, Lori and I. Our fates were sealed together by this one rarity of chance, the role of the genetic dice.

Finally, I reached the school and parked my car. I jumped out and ran into the building. Stunned for a moment, I then went inside the building. "Where is she?" I demanded, bursting my way through students and teachers into the nurse's office. I didn't wait for the nurse to answer. I just followed my daughter's cries for help to the back room.

Lori was lying on a cot, her legs drawn up to her chest. "It hurts so bad, Mom. I just can't stand it any more!"

I sat beside her, rubbing her forehead, trying to calm her down enough to tell me what was going on. The pain was too acute to be the flu. "I need to know exactly what kind of pain it is and precisely where it's coming from so I can help you, dear. Is it here?" I pressed my hand on the left side of her lower abdomen where appendix pain is usually centered and quickly released my hand.

"No, not there," she screamed. "It feels like I'm on fire inside. I want to go home."

"Do you think you can walk to the car if I help you, Lori?"

"I'll try, Mommy."

This was the moment Dr. Stewart had warned me about, the one to watch for. I had always prayed it would never come.

Lori's body quaked with tremors all the way home. The pain was still bad, but it had tired her so much she no longer had the strength to scream. I pulled the car into the driveway and came around to the passenger side to help her out. I couldn't carry her. She was too heavy for me. I knocked on the front door yelling, "Tim! Come help me! Lori's very sick!" I ran back to the car. Tim came out and ran towards me. When he saw Lori's condition the color drained from his face. "Oh my God! Is it. . . ?"

I shook my head affirmatively. "I think so." We got Lori inside. Then I walked over to the phone and dialed the doctor's number.

"Hello, I need to speak to Dr. Stewart right away. This is Tammy Evans. It's an emergency!"

The voice on the other end of the line sounded slow and far too mechanical for me. "Dr. Stewart is in surgery right now. If you have a medical emergency, please call the hospital emergency room at. . . ."

"You don't understand. I believe my daughter is having a porphyria attack. I need Dr. Stewart!"

"Dr. Stewart is unavailable. If you would like to schedule an appointment. . . ."

I slammed the receiver down before she could finish her robotic message. "This is ridiculous!" I went back over to Lori whom Tim had placed on the sofa. She looked deathly pale, and I was scared. I took a deep breath, hoping to be able to think straight and take the appropriate action.

"What should I do, hon?" Tim asked, looking to me for guidance. "Is it porphyria? I heard you talking to Dr. Stewart's office."

"I'm very afraid it is." I tried to think. "Get my glucose tablets out of the cupboard," I said. "We have to make her take as many as she can stomach. She can wash them down with some soda. Then I'm going to see if I can get hold of that new doctor in the one town that Mother's using. Tatum, I think his name is."

Dr. Tatum was young, having recently opened his own family practice and lived close to my parent's house. My mother had heard about him from some friends and decided to go and see him about handling her porphyria. With her attacks coming so close together, she needed someone close by who would be willing to treat her. After their initial consultation, he agreed to take her as a patient. I went with her once, and we had talked.

Dr. Tatum didn't know a lot about porphyria, but he was willing to learn. He was current with the medical aspects of the disease and somewhat knowledgeable of the symptoms. He and I spoke for a long time about treatment techniques and the importance of a high carbohydrate diet. Dr. Tatum was extremely interested in my improvement and my method of carbohydrate therapy. Likewise, I was made to feel comfortable by his willingness to listen to patients and incorporate their advice into his treatment. He had even given me his beeper number and now seemed like a good time to use it. Sure enough, he returned my call in less than a minute.

"Yes, this is Dr. Tatum calling."

"Hi, Dr. Tatum. This is Tammy Evans. I have an emergency on my hands."

"Are you going into an attack, Tammy?" He sounded a little panicky. "It's not me, Dr. Tatum. It's my daughter, Lori. I think she's having a porphyria attack." I explained Lori's symptoms to him and how quickly they had come. "Tim's feeding her glucose tablets now. I checked her pulse and it's one twenty-four."

He didn't answer for what seemed like a very long time. "Has she ever had an episode like this before?"

"Lori's always had severe headaches and recurring stomach cramps, but nothing like this."

He paused again. I was beginning to realize that he didn't know what to do either. "Why don't you keep pushing the carbohydrates and watch her over the next couple of hours. If she gets any worse, call me back and I'll meet you at the hospital," he suggested. "I can't do any testing for the porphyria there, but we could hook up an IV and get the sugar into her system a lot quicker. Remember: No other medication. Lori's in high school isn't she?"

"Yes."

"Ah, I see. Then she's just getting into the age that the symptoms would begin appearing." I hadn't taken the time to think about it, but he was right. My own symptoms, I had come to realize, had begun about the same time.

"Just keep up the carbs and let me know if anything changes."

I returned to Lori's side and watched as Tim hand fed the large white tablets to her. She was able to keep them down, which was a good sign. If she started uncontrollable vomiting, I would have no choice but to take her to the hospital.

"What did he say?" Tim asked.

"He said to keep doing what we're doing and to call him if she gets any worse."

With each sugar tablet and swallow of soda, Lori's pain subsided until she said it was nothing more than a dull ache. After a couple of hours, her heart rate went down almost to a normal pace. The carbohydrates had done their job. Now there was no doubt in my mind that she, too, had to face the curse of porphyria.

I brushed the golden ringlets from Lori's face, seeing the features of the heavenly cherub she had been not so long before. She fell asleep as I stroked her forehead. She was one of the most valuable treasures I had ever been given. I would have gladly taken her suffering and made it my own, but I knew that wasn't possible.

Tim massaged my aching shoulders, watching with me as Lori slept. "I just can't believe this is happening!" I whispered so she would not awaken from my angry words. Tears of rage dripped onto my clenched fists as my entire being shook furiously. "I can handle just about anything, Tim. You know that. But this?"

"I know, hon. She's your daughter." He held me close.

"She's *our* daughter."

"I don't care what I have to do. Whatever it takes! I'm going to make those doctors listen to me," I whispered through my tears. "If I have to scare them, or embarrass them, or even threaten them to do something about porphyria, then that's exactly what I'm going to do."

"You're absolutely right, Tam. We can't go on like this. We have to pull the medical professionals' heads out of the sand." Tim lifted my chin and gazed into my swollen, tear-filled eyes. "And right now, I truly believe you're the only one that can make them do it."

I nodded. "I have to."

For the time being I would have to devote my days to the full recovery of my child. Although she lay resting comfortably right now, I knew porphyria was not finished with her yet. It would not discontinue its attack on her until it had drained nearly every ounce of life force, making room for its own brand of fear to dwell inside of her. Only after the fire that gushed through her veins subsided could I plan my attack. When the electrical buzzing in her limbs and the ferocious waves of nausea had calmed themselves, then I would have the time to devote my entire being to end the terror of porphyria.

Lori had one advantage over her aggressor that neither I nor my mother had possessed. It was the strength of her youth, the resilience of her otherwise perfect body. Several days after her initial attack, she experienced the classic rash of tiny red spots all over her body. It had been inevitable that they would appear, but I hoped and prayed before their arrival that they would present themselves in places that could be hidden by her clothing. I didn't want her to have to endure the embarrassment and shame of appearance, the discrimination and ridicule, I had been forced to most of my life. As if in answer to my prayers, they confined themselves to her back and chest, with a few stragglers lingering in strands down her arms and legs. Although it was little comfort, Lori resigned herself to accept the last of the unusual symptoms. She had seen them on me, in places on my body that cannot be conveniently shielded from the gawking of others. We were both thankful and relieved that the beauty of her facial features would not have to be marred by the gruesome plague, not this time, anyway.

"I think I'm going to try to go back to school tomorrow, Mom," she informed me a week after her episode.

"Are you sure?" I asked, hesitating to agree. "I can pick up more of your work if you don't feel you're ready yet."

"Yeah, I'm sure. It's time, Mom."

"But, sweetheart, you're still so weak!" I tried to reason with her. As soon as the words came out of my mouth, I realized how futile they were. Lori knew her limitations. She was well aware of the strength and endurance that had been sapped from her body and spirit. I did not need to remind her.

"I can't stay cooped up in this house forever, Mom! I need to get back to my routine, get back into life!" Her expression displayed a firm stance of stubborn defiance, not to me, but to her attacker. "I know I'll have to be careful and take it easy the first few days, but I think I can do it. I need to do it!"

My little girl had learned more in the past week of her suffering and pain than I had gleaned from a lifetime of it. I envied her unwavering power of vitality. In a way, it was as if she had read my thoughts that first day of her attack, the ones of anger and confrontation I had posed to the messenger of this illness. Lori possessed the uncommon power within her soul to defeat the shame of this disease she had unwillingly illustrated to her peers.

"All right then. You can go back to school." I wrapped my arms around her. "Just remember, if it gets to be too much, if you feel you can't handle it, you call me and I'll come right away and get you," I reassured her. "But I agree with your decision."

"Yes, Lori," I added. "It is time for *both* of us to get back into life." I looked at her and smiled. "For your education to continue and for me to put aside all spineless frailty and shatter the myth that porphyria is a family curse. It is time for me to fight."

Chapter 15

To Be or
Not to Be

It was twilight. I sat in the kitchen drinking a hot cup of cocoa, pondering my circumstance, my mother's, brother's, and now, Lori's. For as long as I could remember, though I hadn't known its name, this plague had dominated my family's existence. Porphyria was a mysterious killer that slowly plundered its victim, catching the unarmed off guard, taking as much as it can in a single attack, regrouping and then attacking again. Finally all that is left of its prey is the acceptance of death.

My mother doesn't feel the same way I do about porphyria. I'm not sure she allows herself to have an opinion about it. Until recently, Mother had locked this monster away. It was something for her to hide, to keep secret. Her illness represented weakness and lack of control in her life, the two things she feared most. She was alone with her fears, not even understanding what they were, but I cannot cower and hide, especially now that Lori has been stricken.

There are so many questions and no one seems able to

answer them. I have found out very little. I cannot compre-
hend why there seems such a dirth of information, only
closed doors, confused expressions, total ignorance, or fear
of involvement.

"I'm sorry. There's nothing I can do to help you."

"You know more about this disease than I or any other
doctor could tell you."

"For the moment, you seem to have the symptoms
under control. I'm afraid that is the best you will ever be able
to hope for."

The only answers seem to be the ones I continue to
search for within myself. There doesn't even seem to be
really good guesses or suggestions. Trial and error is the
only way. The handful of doctors I've met, who have come
in contact with the disease, know even less about por-
phyria than Mom and I, and they admit it. The general
public is ignorant of its existence.

In an earlier time some members of British royalty such
as George III and, some speculate, Queen Victoria had been
plagued with porphyria. They dubbed it "the Royal Malady."
Perhaps it is fortunate that such an influential family was
afflicted with the disease. Otherwise, I fear, modern medicine
would not even be aware of its existence today. In the pre-
Christian and early church eras, porphyriacs were thought to
be vampires and werewolves. That is why the disease is called
by laymen, "The Vampire's Disease." Although my symptoms
greatly resemble that of a vampire, that certainly doesn't
include the desire to drink warm human blood!

My mother has been ill much of her adult life. Her
attacks come closer together these days, hardly giving her a
chance to recover before the next one strikes. She is too tired

to pursue the search for answers. Even if she wasn't, I don't think she would. My brother denies the fact that he even has porphyria. Unfortunately, he will have to experience a life-threatening attack before he will admit having the disease.

But I can't hide.

For me the question has become, what kind of action should I take? How can I become an advocate for a cure for porphyria? There seems little doubt that, unless a cure is found quickly, my mother, my brother and I will eventually die from porphyria. There are no miracle drugs or New Age treatments to save our lives. There are no choices for us. Still, I must fight for the future of Lori and my other children, for my future grandchildren, and for the people I have never even met who are plagued with this dreaded disorder. I will myself cautiously step onto the narrow path of crusader. Perhaps, I tell myself, this is my destiny.

Tomorrow I'll find out how to register a foundation for this disease. Tomorrow I will pursue every doctor I've ever seen, and those I haven't, until they can no longer turn me away! Tomorrow I will write to the Department of Health and Human Services and beg them for help in having this disease recognized and researched by the medical community. Tomorrow I will talk to anyone who will listen in hopes that someone will respond. I may not obtain the answers I so desperately need right away, and maybe not even in my lifetime. But, someday, the right someone will hear this voice in one form or another. They will see me standing up and shouting, "Hey you, look at me! My daughter and I need your help!" They will recognize our pain and they will have the courage and the knowledge to take it away.

Dr. Stewart had told me in my first visit that there

were no support groups for porphyria, no foundations for research accessible to the public. It seemed to me that here would be a logical place to start. My first plan was to initiate a foundation, a non-profit organization whose purpose would be to collect donations for research and patient information. However, after discussing the idea with my mother, our family's business advisor, I had to abandon my hopes for such a grandiose scheme. Instituting a foundation would take months of legal wrangling and a large amount of money, neither of which I could afford.

"Tammy, I have an idea," my mother said excitedly. "Why don't you go to the county courthouse and register your porphyria organization as a 'doing business as' agency. Every business in the country goes through this process simply to register their activities with the government...it's a first step."

Her suggestion switched on the light bulb in my own head. My brother had gone through the same procedure years before when he started up a small music store. The simple process wouldn't give me the privilege of raising money for research, but it would register my cause as a legitimate organization. It was a start, and with the minuscule five dollar registration fee, it was an affordable solution. I walked out of the courthouse with an exhilarating feeling of accomplishment. The Porphyria Education and Awareness Association was now a reality, even though I was its one and only member.

"Hey there! What have you been up to today?" Tim said, greeting me when I came home.

My husband, comfortably seated in his favorite recliner, was reading the newspaper after a long day on the job. I debated how to explain what I had been up to. After several moments of silent deliberation while I hung up my coat and removed my boots, I decided it best to show him rather than tell l him.

"What's this?" he said, startled. Glancing over his shoulder, I read the words to myself once again.

The county of Alpena hereby issues notification that The Porphyria Education and Awareness Association is licensed and authorized to do business as such.

A shiny gold seal, along with the date and signature of the county clerk at the bottom of this precious document, made it official. This was the first step for the people out there, just like me, who were sick with a disease that no one knew anything about. In an emergency situation, it had become apparent that someone with porphyria could die because of doctor ignorance and lack of information. The situation was so bad that it seemed incomprehensible to me that I had found one physician who knew more than just the basic, observable facts.

"Sweetheart, I think its a wonderful idea!" Tim assured me. "You've been trying so hard to find some sort of help and have come up empty handed each time. As I told you before, someone is going to have to do something for people with this disease. I honestly believe that you are that someone. I am curious about something, though."

"What's that?" I asked.

"What, exactly, is the purpose of the association? I mean, what are your goals?"

I slipped the document back in my purse. "We are going to use it to get information out to professionals whose ignorance has doubled the pain of porphyria sufferers. The first thing I'm going to have to do is draw up some sort of organizational pamphlet that explains what porphyria is. I was thinking of having it printed up on lavender paper. That would trigger people's association of porphyria as the purple poison. You know, what the symptoms are and how one should go about being tested for it. I won't have much to go on. The only information I had was the little Dr. Stewart had given me, and my own experiences, of course."

Looking at the certificate, Tim continued, "this certainly will get people's attention once they see it. I'm sure that when you have a few members, the group can work together to find a solution to porphyria. But...."

"But what?" I countered anxiously. I could tell he wanted to tell me his hidden reservations, but didn't know how to express his thoughts to me without shooting my ideas down.

A few silent minutes passed.

"That was the second part I had a question about," he said wincing. "Don't get me wrong. I really do like the idea of the association and the pamphlet. I'm just wondering how you're going to get this information out to the public. What means of advertising or...um...publicity will you use?"

This was a dilemma indeed. The only method of reaching large portions of the population was through the media: newspapers, television, etc. Everything I had done up to this point was fairly simple and I could remain in the background. I didn't want the association to be about me; I wanted it to be about stopping ignorance about porphyria and ending the mistreatment of its victims. There wasn't the slightest desire within me to become the poster person for this disease. Deep down, I knew that being an advocate for such a cause required a strong voice to speak out, taking the risk of offending people in high places, like the medical community. There was no one else I knew who would do this. No one else had so much at stake.

Somehow, I would have to put aside my reservations about appearing before the public, so the message could be heard.

"I guess Sharon and I'll have to start making phone calls to the TV stations," I said, answering him. "I'll call them, and keep calling them until someone gives me the opportunity to state my cause."

A smile of approval turned up in the corners of Tim's mouth. It was the answer I was hoping he would give me.

Chapter 16

Not Enough People Are Dying

Sitting at my home computer, I began to review the list of a hundred or so state and federal politicians who belonged to health committees. It seemed like an endless task, trying to figure out from their brief biographical statements to which ones I should send follow-up letters. A stack of my newly printed foundation pamphlets stood at my side.

Sharon had been on the kitchen phone for hours, calling one magazine and news program after the other. Each of her requests to speak to a reporter had failed. "No, you don't understand. I want to speak to an investigative reporter. I just told you what the purpose of my call was. I need to find some-one to do a story on a mysterious illness that people are dying from! No, I'm not a celebrity. I'm an ordinary person, just like you. No! No, please, don't hang up! Why you little twerp!"

"Sharon?" I yelled out to her. "You okay in there?" Sharon was committed to curing porphyria, but her high energy could lead her overboard, another thing I had to worry about.

"Name a movie star for me, Tammy. Go ahead, pick anyone you want."

"What on earth are you talking about?"

Sharon stomped into the living room. For a moment I thought I actually saw steam rolling out of her ears. "The only way I'm ever going to get someone on the other end of this phone is to pretend I'm a dying actress!" she proclaimed. "I'd have to fight them off with a pitchfork if I told them that!"

Before I could say anything, she stomped back into the kitchen and started dialing again.

Tim walked through the front door, his arms loaded down with two large cardboard boxes. "How's it going? Any luck yet?" He set the boxes down carefully.

"Not yet, hon," I said. "Sharon finally got through to a real live reporter about an hour ago. He said he'd call back after he did a little digging on porphyria, but he probably won't. She's still in there trying." I looked at Tim with a sheepish grin. "Hey, think of the name of a famous movie actress for me!"

"What?"

"Oh, never mind," I said. Tim shook his head in bewilderment as I started going over the contents of the boxes. "Were you able to get it all?"

"There are exactly one hundred copies of the article and your letters in that box." He looked at his watch. "Can I go out and play now?" he said peevishly.

I patted him on the head and gave him a quick kiss on the cheek. "Three hours and that's it!" I firmly commanded. "I'm going to need your help to get all the packages to the post office before it closes."

"Thanks, Tam!" He swirled around me and scooped

up his golf bag with lightning speed. He knew he had to get out of the driveway before I changed my mind and found more chores for him to do. Tim had been working as hard as Sharon and I, running errands all over town so we could continue our calls. He had certainly earned a few hours of relaxation!

"No! This time I'm putting *you* on hold!" Sharon felt powerful pushing the call-waiting button. "What!" she screamed at the next caller. "Yes, this is Sharon Bruce. Who's this?" Her begruntled expression drained, making room for one of childlike excitement. "Why, of course you can speak with Mrs. Evans." She spoke calmly, waving me over to the phone. "One moment please."

"Hello?"

"Mrs. Evans, this is Jesse Fraley. Sharon Bruce called me earlier about your story."

"Yes, Mr. Fraley?"

"Well, I was very interested in what she had to say, so I did some checking around on this paphoria."

"That's por*phy*ria, Mr. Fraley." I corrected him.

"Yes. Well, anyway, after I contacted a few sources, I decided I'd have to decline doing a feature on it."

"And why is that?" I asked.

"I assure you, it's nothing personal, but there's just not enough people out there...well, um, dying of it to make it newsworthy."

I couldn't believe what I was hearing! "Tell me, Mr. Fraley, just how many people need to die, or be sick with a disease before the public gets to find out about it? A thousand? Ten thousand? How about a million? Would that be enough, Mr. Fraley?"

"Look, I'm really sorry. . . ."

"No, I don't think you are. But, I can guarantee you this, Mr. Fraley, you will be someday!"

I slammed the phone back on its base and walked out of the kitchen furious over the ignorance of his comments. I sighed deeply to gain my composure. "He said there weren't enough people dying of porphyria to make it newsworthy!"

Sharon slid down into the chair and stared at me in disbelief.

"I don't get it, Sharon! What in the world are we going to have to do to get someone to publicize what's going on with this disease? All we want is one story. One stinking national news story to make people aware of what's going on."

I was at my wits' end. How could we educate and promote awareness of porphyria if no one would listen? *Is everyone, like this wet-nosed jerk of a reporter, telling me it is all for nothing?* I wondered. "What's it going to take to make them listen? Am I going to have to walk a thousand miles to get my point across, or what?"

Sharon watched in complete amazement as I paced back and forth in front of her, spewing anger. Just then, it hit me.

"That's it!" My eyes lit up.

"What are you talking about? What's *it*?"

Yes, that's exactly what I'm going to do, I thought, reasoning with myself. There'll be no way for them to ignore me then.

"What?" Sharon hollered at me.

"Sharon! I'm going to *walk*!"

"That just might do it."

Sharon was right. Our announcement of the walk intrigued at least one reporter, Janeene Taylor of the *Evening*

Star. When I got on the phone she made an appointment to interview me the next evening.

"I think I'll just lay down for a while if you don't mind, Sharon."

"What time are you supposed to be in Petoskey to meet the reporter for the interview?" Tim asked, as he entered the room, back from his golf game.

Sharon looked out the sliding glass door. The wind was starting to pick up, piling the snow into drifts around the house. "It's not until eight, but I think we'd better leave a little earlier than we planned."

"All right," I said, kicking off my shoes and climbing into bed. I couldn't keep my eyes open any longer. Although I was feeling somewhat better, I tired easily.

"You just get some sleep. I'll make us a light lunch."

I drifted off to sleep thinking of the interview. For months I had been working on setting up the foundation, writing up pamphlets, trying to get the media to promote it. Nothing had happened, and it had been discouraging. But now I had an interview with the *Evening Star*. It was not a large newspaper, but it was a beginning.

When I woke up, Sharon was sitting on a chair in the bedroom. It seemed like I had only been asleep for a brief moment. However, from the darkening sky, I could tell that it was obviously later in the afternoon.

"How long have I been asleep?"

She didn't answer, but walked over to the door.

"Sharon, what's wrong?" I said, crawling out of bed. She was silent. I walked over to where she was standing and took a look. As soon as I looked outside, I understood. There was nothing to see. A thick swirling cloud of white obscured all of the buildings, the trees and the lake, all of which had been visible a few short hours ago. It was the first blizzard of the season, and neither Sharon nor I could see two feet in front of us.

"I'd better call Janeene and tell her we won't be able to make it." One look outside was enough to change my travel plans. I was a sissy when it came to driving in stormy conditions. Ice was my biggest fear.

"We'll be okay," Sharon whispered. She was still staring at the storm.

I turned around and looked at her. "Are you crazy? It's a total whiteout, Sharon! We won't even make it out of our driveway let alone fifty miles on a two-lane road!"

Tim came into the room and heard our conversation. "If you leave now that gives you four hours to get there on time. You're never going to get another opportunity like this, Tammy. You have to go," he said.

My reclusive lifestyle because of the humiliation of porphyria had been my safety net. My home was always there for me to fall on if I felt ill, if something went wrong, if someone made fun of how I looked or acted. However, in just a few short hours, I was going to give my first interview, after which everyone could see me and judge my words. My life was about to change in a dramatic way, and my safety net was nowhere to be found. If I fell, I would fall hard, and it would hurt.

"I'm scared," I said to Tim and Sharon. "Maybe not a single soul will be the least interested in my fight against my family's illness. If this happens, I will be right back where I started, alone and unsure where next to turn for help."

Tim zipped the suitcase and placed it next to the door. Then he walked over to me. His arms drew me close to him and held me in that special way that always made me feel like the most important person in the world. "No matter what happens as a result of this, I want you to know how proud I am of you. I know this hasn't been easy. There have been times when you felt like giving up. I think that's fairly normal, but you have to fight Tammy. It's the only way."

"I feel like it would be less frightening to just run away and hide right now," I confided in him.

"Would it?" he asked. "Would it really be easier to know that you had the opportunity to help others who have porphyria and you let it slip away because you were afraid of what people will think of you?"

His words stung my heart with a piercing blow of harsh reality. Tim had fostered the birth of a new spirit within me. He had stood by and supported me as I stopped hiding and took the first steps toward becoming a different kind of person. Now I realized that he was giving up much more than I was. I would no longer be a private person, his loving wife. My crusade, if it succeeded, would take me further and further away at times from him. Yet, Tim was willing to let me go because he felt what I was doing was important for Lori, for me and others. He was willing to put aside his own desires as well as his fears about my future because he felt I had found the right path.

"Thank you," I whispered.

"For what?"

"For helping me step through the door. For loving me through the best and worst of times."

I quickly got dressed while Sharon heated the car.

After twenty miles and two hours of driving down a road we couldn't see, our courage was beginning to look a lot more like stupidity. We knew the shoreline of Lake Michigan was only a few yards to our left, while rocky tree-lined foothills loomed to our right. The two landmarks had been our only source of navigation but, as darkness set in, they were no longer visible. For a while, there had been the tail lights of a vehicle in front of us to follow, but the driver had turned off, leaving us alone and feeling lost. In defeat, Sharon pulled off to what she hoped was the shoulder of the road.

"I'm sorry, Tammy. I just can't see anymore. We're going to have to wait here until it blows over."

From the weather report on the car radio, we both knew that wasn't going to happen for at least another forty-eight hours. It was a bad storm, one we had no business being out in. Sharon ran the car motor and heater at intervals so we wouldn't get too cold. Both of us wondered silently how we were going to get ourselves out of such a foolish predicament.

"Here." Sharon grabbed the wool blanket out of the back seat and threw it over us. "Well, go ahead and say it: Stupid, stupid, stupid!"

That was the only word to describe what we had done. But I had to giggle. Since we had become so close, we were always getting ourselves into one scrape after the other. Somehow, we always managed to get through with a smile on our faces.

"Yeah, you'll get your newspaper headline. I can see it now! 'They Died on Their Way to Have an Interview With Me,' by Janeene Taylor," Sharon laughed.

"What was that?"

I heard something outside the car. It sounded like a

twig scraping against the window.

"You're hallucinating, Tammy!"

"No! Listen! There it is again."

She heard the noise that time, too. We squinted to see into the darkness, but there appeared to be nothing. Suddenly, the dim beam of a flashlight broke through the wall of blinding snow. "Are you ladies all right in there?" The beefy uniform-clad figure rubbed a peephole through the icy glaze on the window. It was the sheriff! We were saved!

Sharon wasted no time in explaining our predicament. "Look, officer, I know it's crazy, but she's got to be in Petoskey for an interview. Can we follow you into town?"

"I can take you to the county line, but you're on your own after that."

We accepted his offer. Sharon got a cocky look on her face. "See, Tammy, I knew everything would be fine." We started laughing, but inside we still were afraid we weren't going to make it.

Finally, the hazy glow of Petoskey's street lights loomed in the distance. The sheriff's car was still ahead of us, leading the way. Another mile up the road we passed the city limit sign, where he turned his car around and headed back into the darkness we had just traveled. We yelled out our thanks to him as he passed by us and disappeared into the blackness.

"Sharon, I think we just met an angel!"

Janeene Taylor was waiting in the front booth of the restaurant when we arrived. Her jolly, whimsical exterior matched the voice I had spoken with on the telephone days before. She welcomed us to her temporary office, surprised that we showed up at all.

"I was just about to leave when you walked in. I didn't think you'd risk coming all that way in this weather," she said. "Please sit down. You look like you could use a hot meal."

Sharon and I ordered the special, turkey with dressing. We were thankful to be safe and to eat something warm. Janeene pulled a spiral steno pad from her briefcase and pulled her gold-rimmed glasses down from where they rested on top of her head.

"I have an idea for the story I want to tell about you. Of course, I'll want to add as many details as possible about the disease and your new foundation. But I'd like our readers to get a feel for the woman behind the story. You know, give it a personal, heartwarming theme. Is that all right with you?"

Her idea surprised me. I never considered that anyone would want to know how I felt about what was happening to me.

"I'm also going to be interviewing Dr. Stewart. I want to get his view on what it feels like not to be able to heal a patient."

"It's doubtful he'll talk of that, don't you think? I don't know of any doctor who would be willing to admit he or she can't heal someone," I said.

"That's exactly what I want to write about," she said. "I think it's important to expose that problem in your struggle as a patient with a serious disease. I want to show how doctors need to change their attitudes."

I smiled. Janeene possessed the insight to reveal more than just the facts. Her sensitivity caused me to like her right away, to think about things in a different way. She slid her pen at a rapid pace across each page as I rambled on about my illness and the walk we planned. The emotions flowed out of me, one after the other. Fear, resentment, loneliness, embarrassment: She wrote it all down.

"Tammy, I want you to tell me a little about your daughter."

I didn't understand what she wanted me to say. What feelings was she attempting to dig out of me?

"She has porphyria, too," I started to say.

"I know she does, but that's not what I want. I need you to tell me how you felt when you went to the school that day and realized your daughter had the symptoms of porphyria."

My freely expressed opinions stopped. Janeene was asking me to tell her something too personal. Those were feelings that were too private, too raw. Then I started speaking without a plan, just telling her about Lori. "At first I felt like my life had been crushed. And then I felt angry, angry that my child had been afflicted and everyone knew so little about what to do. And that anger made me want to fight."

"Tammy, I have another personal question. How did you feel when you were lying in the hospital bed and realized your mother had suspected all along what was wrong with you?"

I blanched, my heart began racing. Despite the fact that I was once again speechless, Janeene's pen continued to write. She was capturing my reaction in her notes. Without another word about it, she moved on to something else. Janeene had produced the effect she had intended without me uttering a sound.

It was a long interview, carrying on even after the waitress cleared away our dinners. Afterward, I shared my scrapbook with Janeene, letting her read the letters I had received and the foundation materials. Sharon pulled her camera out of her purse. "How about I get a picture of the two of you for the scrapbook?" Janeene and I complied, posing in different ways for each shot. Then Janeene took some pictures of me standing alone for her article.

"The story should appear in the paper two days from today. I'll be sure to send you a copy after it comes out." I liked Janeene and she seemed to like me, too. "When you're ready to begin the trek, give me a call. Maybe we can do a follow-up."

"Thank you, Janeene. You've been so kind. I can't wait to see what you end up writing about porphyria and me."

We gave each other a hug. It seemed like the proper goodbye, since we had become so close during these hours. "We'd better leave soon, Sharon. It looks like it's letting up a little bit. We should take advantage of the break in the storm."

Janeene was horrified. "You aren't driving back tonight, are you?"

"We'll be okay, Janeene. God got us here in one piece. He'll get us back."

"I'll pray for you," she said.

The snowplows had been out while we were in the restaurant. Only light, feathery flakes were falling on the patchy road before us. We would have to hurry, though. The radio predicted more gusty winds on the way.

"You did very well, especially on the questions about Lori, which I know were hard for you," Sharon said. "I noticed you kind of choked when she asked about your mother."

"What was I supposed to tell her? She's my mother, Sharon. I can't tell a reporter that I think my mother was wrong to keep porphyria a secret from me."

"I think you just answered your own question, Tammy. Just like doctors and patients, families need to talk about important things together. You and your mother need to talk this out."

"You're right, but it's never going to happen. Lately, Mom and I have talked in generic terms about the symptoms of porphyria, but she never discussed how she felt about it. Mom doesn't have the kind of personality that would allow her to be open with her emotions that way. I don't like that about her, but I have learned to accept it. I have you and Tim if I need to talk. That will have to be enough."

We made it home, but it was a long, difficult trip. I begged Sharon to sleep over. Neither one of us was tired. The evening had been too eventful to just climb into bed and go to sleep. She consented and the three of us, Tim, Sharon and I, sat up talking for hours. We all couldn't wait to see the finished article.

When the big day finally came, Tim, Sharon and I sat at the breakfast table, drinking coffee and reading the article Janeene had written.

"Listen to this," I said. "'She first heard of the disease while in a hospital bed in Petoskey. Her mother, who secretly suffered with the disease for years, spoke up.'" Janeene had managed to allude to it without me saying a word.

"Sounds ominous," Tim commented.

"Here's a quote from Dr. Stewart. 'We go into the business to cure people. The bottom line is, we can't cure everybody. This is basically her disease. She's going to have to live with it.'"

I read on. "Here's one from me about going to Lori's school and seeing her and realizing that she too had the disease."

Tim put his coffee cup down and took the paper from
me. "Let me see. Ah, Lori. That was the worst part of all this
for you, honey, wasn't it?"

I nodded. Tears formed in my eyes.

Tim continued to scroll down the page. "Well, overall,
I think Janeene did a fine job. It isn't her fault she couldn't
get any emotion out of Dr. Stewart," he said. "The main thing
is, she's getting the word out for us."

I stuffed the newspaper into my scrapbook and started
running water into the sink to wash the morning dishes. The
phone rang.

"Mrs. Evans?"

The male voice was unfamiliar to me.

"Yes. How can I help you?"

"This is Charles Harris of WLRI T.V. We'd like to
interview you on *Good Morning, Michigan.*"

"Cue music!" The young man's voice shouted
from beyond the glaring white light. Immediately the
noisy, clattering jingle echoed through the tiny sound-
proof room.

"And cue intro!" he shouted again. I heard the muffled recorded voice of the television announcer. I could not
decipher his words from where they were taping in the
next room.

"And, three, two, one." A pointed finger jolted out
from behind the camera directly at the long laminated bar I
was seated behind.

"Good morning, everyone, and thank you for joining
me for today's edition. My name is Rachel Milostin, and I'll
be your host." The tall, raven-haired woman sitting next to

me paused briefly. It was a rehearsed pause. I could tell she had done it a hundred times before.

"My guest today is Tammy Evans." Rachel turned to me. "Thank you for joining us today, Tammy. You must have had quite a drive all the way from Alpena in that snowstorm."

"I didn't want to miss this broadcast. It's very important. Thank you for having me, Rachel." I didn't know if I should use up my allotted fifteen minutes to discuss the weather, or just let it slide.

Rachel smiled politely and turned back toward the camera. "Tammy is with us today to discuss one of the most life-threatening diseases known to modern medicine." She swiveled her stool toward me once more. "And Tammy, it must be rare because I had never heard of it before you were scheduled to be with us. Could you please pronounce the name of the disease for our audience at home?"

I knew I was in television land now. I had never quite heard porphyria described that way before. What a hook!

"Certainly, Rachel. The name of the disorder is porphyria. As far as it being rare, I would have to say that the term 'rarely diagnosed' would better describe it."

"Tammy, you were diagnosed with porphyria last year at the Wyatt Clinic by Dr. Jonathan Stewart. Why don't you just give us a brief description of what you have and how you came to be diagnosed."

The ball was in my court now. It was my one and only chance to accomplish what I had come there to do. I wasn't really sure where I should direct my attention, to the camera, or to Rachel. In a split second, I chose Rachel. I told her the story about my hospital stay, the endless testing, and the last resort, my daughter having the disease. She nodded every so

often to show her interest, making appropriate groans and
"ahs" where they fit in. I explained the symptoms of porphyria in somewhat graphic detail. I was hesitant about
doing it, but Sharon had said it was the best direction to take
to capture the audience's attention. From behind the camera,
the hand appeared again, holding up a white cardboard sign
that read "one minute." I began to talk of the Trek for Truth
and explain the whys, where and when.

"It sounds like an incredible adventure, Tammy!"

Rachel turned toward the camera again. "And we wish
you good luck. The Trek for Truth, in case you want to root
Tammy on, will take place. . . ." Her voice droned on for a
few minutes, reiterating the time and place until the hand
behind the camera held up another placard and Rachel said
smoothly, "We'll be back with more of Tammy Evans's story.
Please stay with us."

The masculine voice emanated from the bright light
again. "That's it. You're clear for commercial."

I didn't dare move until Rachel did. To my surprise,
she jumped off the stool and started adjusting her skirt. "I
hate wool! It's always so itchy!"

The men who had been shouting commands came out
from behind the lights and hovered around the makeshift set.
"You did great, Tammy! If I didn't know better, I'd say you
were a professional," one of them complimented me.

"Thank you." I looked past him to where Sharon was
standing in the corner. She had a big smile on her face and
was giving the thumbs-up sign.

"Tammy, for the second half of the program I'm just
going to ask you one question and you can take it from
there," Rachel said. "When it's time to wrap it up, I'll touch

your arm lightly to signal you."

"That sounds good," I said.

"I can't believe you're not nervous or anything! Most of my guests stutter a lot or lose their train of thought. Even I was scared to death the first time I got in front of the camera!" Rachel hopped back onto the stool and clipped her microphone back on her sweater.

"I don't know. It doesn't really seem like I'm on television. I feel more like I'm sitting in someone's kitchen talking about what has become the focus of my life." Other than the bright lights that were beginning to make my eyes water and sting, that was exactly what it felt like.

Suddenly everyone scattered from sight. I heard the voice again, "And, three, two, one." Then the finger shot out at us.

"Welcome back to the second half of our program. We're talking with Tammy Evans, the founder and director of the Porphyria Education and Awareness Foundation who will soon be undertaking a walk for her cause. Tammy, tell us a little bit about your foundation and what it is you hope to accomplish by the walk."

It was the first opportunity I had to explain in public what my agenda was. It was so important to get it just right.

"The foundation was set up for several different reasons, Rachel. First and foremost, our goal is to give others who have porphyria a place to contact with their questions and concerns. I don't have all the answers. But, from my own personal experience, I know how important it is to have someone to talk to, someone who can relate to what they are going through." So far, so good! "Our second reason for existing is to educate physicians to the symptoms of porphyria. As I described

before, they are numerous. Quite often, they portray themselves as indications of other, more common ailments. Medical
students should be required to undertake a more in-depth study
of the porphyrias rather than just a cursory glance at it, as they
do now. Those who are already practicing need to listen to their
patients when they describe multiple symptoms. They need to
look at the whole picture before making a diagnosis. By learning
to do this, they could very well prolong, perhaps even save,
someone's life."

Rachel touched my arm, just as she promised. "We're
just about out of time, Tammy. Before we go, I want to thank
you for joining us today and wish you luck with your cause
and especially the walk you'll soon be undertaking." She
shook my hand. "For those of you who would like more
information about the Porphyria Education and Awareness
Foundation, you can contact Tammy at the phone number on
the bottom of your screen." Two hands popped out of the
bright lights this time, waving around in small circles. "I am
your host, Rachel Milostin, wishing you safe travel throughout the day. Join us again tomorrow for another edition of
Good Morning, Michigan!"

"And, we're clear!"

Sharon pushed her way through the group of people that
surrounded the stage. "I'm so proud of you!" She hugged me
hard around my neck. At that moment, I was feeling pretty
proud of me, too.

"Yes, me too," Rachel joined in. "Tammy, do you
mind if I ask you a personal question?"

"No, not at all," I replied.

"I was just curious. Do you wear those dark glasses
and that high collar all the time? I mean, do you have to,

because of your skin and the sunlight?" Rachel seemed a little uncomfortable, even embarrassed, for asking.

"Yes, Rachel. I have to." I gave her a lot of credit for being bold enough to confront me. Most people just stared, whispering derogatory remarks behind my back. "But it's okay. I'm not afraid of who I am or what I look like anymore. That's one of the things that I am trying to get across to others. That they don't have to be afraid of us who suffer from porphyria either."

"I think I understand you a little better now." She held out her hand once again for me to shake. "You are a very brave woman, Tammy Evans. And I'm happy to have met you."

"I'm happy to have met you, too, Rachel. Thank you for giving me the opportunity to tell my story."

"Believe me, the pleasure was all mine."

Sharon and I turned to leave. "Tammy?" Rachel called out to me.

"Yes, Rachel?"

"Good luck!"

Chapter 17

The Courage to Stand Alone

My appearance on *Good Morning, Michigan* and Janeene Taylor's article had started the media ball rolling, but there was much to be done to make the walk a reality.

"This is Tammy Evans, director of the Porphyria Education and Awareness Foundation. I'm calling about an event we're having called the Trek for Truth. We'd like to include your organization as sponsors."

The words poured out of my mouth like a recorded message. I had repeated the same statement at least two hundred times.

"The Trek for Truth is a one-hundred-and-twenty-mile walk my daughter and I are embarking on to promote a national awareness for an orphan disease called porphyria which we both have."

"What is porphyria? I've never heard of it before."

"What kind of treatment do you take? Is there a cure?"

My mind was spinning, racing with all of the planning, phone calls, contacts and preparations for what I was about to do. Had I gotten myself in over my head? Perhaps. Probably. Did I actually believe I could walk a hundred and twenty miles? It didn't really matter what I believed anymore. It was something that had to be done!

I was angry with all the media people who implied that my daughter's life was not a reasonable incentive to try to do something about porphyria. I was angry with the medical community which thrived on wallowing in their ignorance. Most of all, I was angry with myself for playing their silly little games for so long. In my naivete, I had trusted the organized powers of our society to fight against porphyria. I had begged them to help me and they hadn't. I had learned one very important lesson. Looking to others to help didn't work. You have to look to yourself.

I wished I could walk across the entire country. However, since my physical condition is so weak at times that would not be possible so I finally decided to walk the one hundred and twenty miles to the front entrance of the Wyatt Clinic. "It will have to be a symbolic walk," I said to Sharon. "We can publicize it as walking across Michigan, from one shore to the other."

Though Tim felt the distance was too much for me, he agreed. In the end, it was Tim who came up with the name for the event. "You have to give it a catchy name so people will have an idea of what you're doing and why you're doing it," he said. "Trek for Truth! I think that says it all."

It was Lori who was the most difficult to convince. She was feeling better. The strength and endurance of youth were helping her rebound from the attack much faster than I ever had. The physical act of walking that far wasn't the part she was having trouble with. It was all the cruelty, indifference and social unconcern she had experienced since it had become known that she had the illness known as "The Vampire Disease." "What makes you think that anyone will care how far we walk? If they don't care if people are dying, they certainly won't bother taking a second look at someone who's walking. We're going to walk all the way to Petoskey and no one will even know we did it!" From all the resistance Sharon and I had met, there was a very good chance Lori was correct in her thinking. But to me it was the only option left. I felt we had to grasp it and try to make our cause known. Besides, Lori now needed to be tested for porphyria and to be seen by Dr. Stewart, as I had. The appointment could be scheduled for the last day of the Trek, adding to the purpose. Eventually, Lori recognized the importance of our making a statement.

The other children saw it as an adventure and wanted to walk with us. While there, they weren't really interested in the cause behind the act. They just thought it was cool to have a week off from school to go hiking.

My mother passed the idea off as another ridiculous concoction of my overactive imagination. "Well, honey, whether you actually ever do it or not, remember that I still love you." It was than I realized the responsibility lay solely with me. I had become a political, human rights, medical, and maternal advocate. It was a role I was not sure I had the fortitude or ability to play. Nevertheless, it was the one I had undertaken.

Sharon had jumped right in to help me. "I won't walk ten feet, let alone a hundred miles." She scrunched up her face. "But I can't let you do all of this alone, either. You're going to need someone to drive the relief vehicle." From that point on, she made phone calls to stores, restaurants and motels on our route asking them to donate meals and lodging. Everywhere she went, she promoted the walk and brought people together to support Lori and me.

It was my own community that ultimately surprised me. People I had never met before and some who had once been cruel to me encouraged and endorsed our trek. By the time Sharon and I completed all of the preliminary preparations, our sponsors numbered over fifty businesses, media, civic and police organizations. Although I appreciated their kind words and commitment, I felt weighted by the responsibility of living up to our goal. I worried constantly that I would become too ill to undertake the walk.

Physically I was having a few warning signs that let me know the disease was still there. The mental confusion I sometimes experienced in the past now became worse. My head pounded constantly. Skin blisters began to appear, first on my body and then on my face. The pain continued. I tried to control my body, but it was becoming more difficult each day. It was going to be a touch-and-go struggle to make the trip. On it, I would have to get through one day at a time. Meanwhile, I concentrated on the carbohydrate diet of which Dr. Stewart had spoken in order to build up my strength as best as I could.

"And how are you ladies doing?" The waitress at the Elks Lodge to which our husbands belonged had been attending to Sharon and me all evening. "Can I get you another soda? Or, how about some supper?"

I looked up briefly from my notes. "Thanks, Dana, but I think we're going to finish up and go home."

"All right. If you change your mind, just give me a holler." She left our table and walked over to the pool table where some men were playing a tournament.

Bob Donally, who headed this lodge, had shown a sincere interest in the Trek the moment he found out about it. Bob wanted to make sure I wore the best walking shoes and that all three of us had matching purple sweatshirts with "Trek for Truth" printed on the back. He approached his committee for funds to provide the items, and they agreed. While Sharon and I sat there working on the details, Bob approached us with another idea.

"I hope I'm not interrupting, but I'd like to swing an idea past you." He pulled up a chair and explained his proposal. "Tammy, do you still need money to cover the cost of Lori's testing and doctor visit as well as the trek?"

I nodded wearily. "Lori's visit to the clinic will be about four hundred dollars and then there's the trek itself." I sighed. "But don't worry, Bob. Tim and I will find a way to take care of it," I told him.

"Well, just hear me out. Tomorrow there will be a country western band playing after our fish fry. Most of the regular members come out when there's music and dancing. You both know how packed it is here on Friday nights." I couldn't tell what he was leading up to. "Anyway, I thought it would be an excellent time for them to show their support of you by donating to your cause."

I shook my head. A fund-raiser was the last thing I wanted to be involved in. If there was some sort of research clinic or national support group to give the money to, that would be fine. However, I would feel greedy asking people

to financially support something that might or might not
produce concrete results. And I didn't want to beg. I
reached over to pat his hand. "That's a very kind gesture,
Bob. But no."

"Now, Tammy," Sharon interrupted. "I think you
should take Bob up on his offer. You need the money and the
members would be more than happy to help you out.
Besides, how are you going to pay those bills if we don't
have a fund-raiser?"

"Just like I always do, a little bit each month until
they're paid off," I snapped.

"You can't do this one all by yourself, Tammy,"
Bob said. "I know medical bills are mounting and
you're not working. Even though Tim does well he must
be feeling squeezed." I nodded. "Please, it would make
all of us feel so good to do our part."

"All right, you guys. I give!"

They both looked pleased with my decision.

"But only on one condition."

"What's that?" Bob asked.

"As soon as we've collected enough money to cover
these costs, we put an end to it. I don't want to take in any
more money than is absolutely necessary."

They nodded in agreement to my request.

"That will be great, Tammy," Bob said. "You'll
see! Now, just before dinner I'll have you come up to
the microphone and announce what you're doing and
what the money will be used for. We can get some bread
baskets from the kitchen to pass around during the
music." He was so excited over his plans. "It's all set
then. I'll see you both tomorrow night."

Sharon saw me pale at Bob's suggestion that I make a
speech. She tried to quell my anxiety. "You have to tell
everyone what it's about, Tammy. They'll have to hear it
from you, not Bob."

"I can't get up in front of a big crowd like that. It
would scare me to death." I was shaking at the thought of
making a live speech.

"You have to do it," she said.

"But they're all strangers. Some of them will look at
me in disgust. Whisper about how I look, like they've
always done."

"No, you'll make them friends just as you did me, and,
don't forget, I'll be with you."

That Friday night I had a bad breakout and had to
cover my body from head to toe. There were at least one
hundred people in the lodge when Lori, Sharon and I
arrived. Mike and Tim were with us. We sat at a table in the
back corner and waited for the waitress to take our orders.
By the time our sodas arrived, people all around us were
staring and whispering behind cupped hands. Even though I
couldn't hear what they were saying, I knew it was my
strange appearance that made them stare and whisper. Their
actions brought back all the rejections I'd suffered through
the years. I felt tense and afraid.

A short while later, Bob Donally walked up to the
bandstand and waved at me to join him. The moment of truth
had arrived. My legs trembled beneath me as I made my way
through the rows of tables. I knew the crowd was watching
me as the entire room hushed into silence. When I reached the
stage, Bob put his hand over the microphone and whispered
in my ear, "Don't worry. Sharon told me how scared you were

to stand up here." He winked at me and put his arm around my shoulder. "We'll get through this together." Suddenly, I felt better. I looked over at my family. They were rooting for me, plus Sharon and now Bob. I stopped trembling.

"Tonight, we have one of our own who would like to say a few words before we eat," Bob began. "As you all know, Tammy and her daughter, Lori, have suffered a serious illness which, as of today, has no cure. They are about to begin a difficult journey on foot. I'm proud of our lodge members for supporting them, but there's still more we need to do. I'll turn the microphone over to Tammy so she can explain."

Bob kept his arm around me to help me forward and held onto me. "Thank you, Bob," I managed to say. The microphone squealed back at me. My heart began pounding inside my chest and I couldn't remember any of the words I'd rehearsed the night before. But there was no backing out now. The crowd, its eyes on me, waited in silence for me to speak. As I took a last-moment look around the room, I remembered Sharon's words: "You'll make them your friends just as you did me."

I smiled.

Then I began talking about porphyria and what it had done to my family. The words came easier now and their faces told me many had become supporters, friends. Finally, I brought my speech to an end.

"I want to thank the lodge for its generous donation of the sweatshirts and shoes. However, tonight I'd like to request one more favor from all of you. As most of you will read in the folders I've given you, funding both this walk and Lori's testing for porphyria will be extremely expensive. I'd like to thank you in advance for any donation you put in the baskets that will be distributed to your tables later this evening. Also, the opening ceremonies for our walk will be next Friday morning at nine o'clock." Now my voice gathered force. "I invite you all to join us as we begin our journey, our Trek for Truth. Thank you."

I got down from the stage as quickly as my bad right foot would allow me and went to my seat. Before I had a chance to get there, Sharon stopped me. The spotlight shone on her. She had a white paint marker in her hand and proceeded to write something on the front of my sweatshirt. When she was finished, I looked down and saw that it read, "Good luck, Tammy! Love, your best friend, Sharon Bruce." All eyes were on her as she placed the first one-dollar bill into the basket on our table.

In the next hour I went from table to table so people could ask me questions about the disease and what it did. After the first few minutes, it wasn't so difficult. By their remarks I learned there were some there who did not believe in me or care about Lori's and my situation. However, their disapproval was, by far, outweighed by those people who did care. There were women and men, young and old, who patted me on the shoulder and said, "We're proud of you!" Tim and Mike remained in the corner of the room, counting out each basket as we brought it to them. By the end of the evening, the people in the room had dwindled down to a few older gentlemen at the bar as Tim was calculating the final amounts. Finally, Tim pushed the buttons of the calculator and announced, "Tammy, you're way over the top!" Sharon and I applauded, and the men at the bar joined in.

We all hugged each other, crying and laughing at the same time. It was then that I realized that Sharon and Bob had been right all along. It was a rewarding feeling to allow those who offered help to give it and to receive their gift in the same spirit it was given.

With only three days to go before the Trek began, the last big task left on our list of things to do was to go over the route and make sure there wouldn't be any unexpected surprises along the way. This morning, Sharon reset the car's odometer and took out pen and paper to record our mileage. "You ready?" she asked, and I got in the car.

M-32 was a two-lane highway running through the heart of northern Michigan. It began on the eastern shore of Lake Huron and ended just west of Gaylord, at the center of the state. In between, a dozen or so quaint villages dotted its path. At Gaylord, we were scheduled to turn on to U.S. 131 which would bring us through Boyne Mountain and on into Petoskey. It was a barren, forty-mile stretch of road with nothing but open fields and, eventually, rolling hills to decorate its landscape. As far as our route was concerned, it wasn't exactly going to be a high profile venture. We had worked hard to drum up publicity in the small towns, sending flyers to all of the businesses along the way. This car trip through them would be our last chance to encourage the residents to join in our crusade.

At each five-mile interval, I watched for a comfortable place along the road for our breaks, writing down the location and description as Sharon drove slowly by. At each motel and restaurant donating their services, we stopped for a few minutes to introduce ourselves and firm up the arrangements. Everyone we talked to was so kind, and even a little excited. We shook their hands and told them to be watching for us. Somehow, I knew they would be.

After each stop, I could feel anticipation building inside of me. It was really going to happen! The excitement was finally beginning to override any doubts I still had.

"You look like you're about to burst with happiness, Tammy," Sharon said.

"In a way, I feel like I may do just that! It's so exciting to imagine that, in just a few days, I'll be walking down these roads handing out purple ribbons and telling people about porphyria," I said.

Sharon laughed at my statement. "Tammy, it doesn't look difficult right now because you're not walking it. We're driving down the road in a car!"

"I know that, Sharon." I looked out the window. "Maybe it's the spring air, or the buds starting to come out on the trees that's making me feel so refreshed and alive. It's going to be a beautiful walk, don't you think?"

Sharon looked up at the sky as if surveying incoming clouds. "I hope, but I'm still concerned that you won't be able to walk this distance with your physical disabilities and possible weather problems."

"I'm going to make it," I said determinedly. "And as for the weather, it would be far worse for me to be out for hours in the sun than in a little bit of rain."

She nodded. "I almost forgot what happens to you in sunlight."

"Most any kind of weather would be more welcome than the hot, glaring rays of the sun," I said. "Lori is not as susceptible to the sunlight as I am, so it isn't as much a concern for her. For me, it would be devastating. Just a few hours of exposure could mean real trouble."

"As long as it doesn't snow," Sharon sighed, "I'll be happy to drive."

I shook my head. "It's the middle of April. There's not much chance of that kind of weather now." Sharon gave me a sphinx-like smile.

The last few miles of our test ride were filled with medium grade foothills that led into the city of Petoskey. They would, in my opinion, be the most difficult part of the trek. That part of U.S. 131 was used as a major thoroughfare by truckers. With all of the twists and turns in the road that took us through the tiny mountains, it had the potential to be a serious safety hazard. I studied the shoulder of the road as we continued on, worrying that it was much narrower than the one on the earlier part of the road.

The beautiful city of Petoskey was situated on the shore of Lake Michigan and surrounded by Little Traverse Bay. Each time I visited, it reminded me of San Francisco with its quaint buildings and old-fashioned street lights. Petoskey was the perfect place to end the Trek for Truth.

"There's the clinic up on your left, Sharon." I pointed the building out to her. "Pull into the driveway and under the arch so I can get the exact mileage."

She stopped the car directly under the massive pillars that supported the large oval sign. WELCOME TO WYATT CLINIC MEDICAL CENTER loomed above our heads in bold white letters. "Wow!" Sharon uttered in awe. "It's really going to be a sight when you finally walk through that gate and under the arch!"

"You mean when *we* walk through it," I corrected her.

She looked confused. "What's this *we* business? I told you, Tammy, I'm not walking."

"I know. But it would mean so much to me if you changed your mind and walked the last mile with Lori and me. Sharon, I won't ask you to walk any other part of the trek if you'll just promise to walk through the arch with us."

"Well, if you put it like that, I'd look pretty foolish turning you down," she said.

We looked at the arch one last time before heading back to Alpena. I prayed for strength and fortitude so that, despite my pain and weakness, I could return to that spot in triumph.

In all, we had accomplished a great deal during this final week of preparations. However, as the hours began ticking away, fear built up inside me about the trek itself. My health was worsening. Sharon saw what was happening to me physically and it scared her too. Until the day before the walk was set to begin, I had done a fairly decent job of hiding it from Tim. That is, until he placed his hand on my back and I shrieked in pain.

"Tammy, you're having an attack," he said worriedly. "You shouldn't do this walk. It might make you worse."

The lesions and boils were multiplying at a rapid pace. The shooting pain that had an eerie way of floating all over my body had situated itself in my right hand. A Vaseline-like film coated my eyes, preventing me from seeing clearly. My heart rate hadn't been under one fifteen for over a week. With all of this, I felt like a human time bomb!

If I had let Tim know about any of the symptoms earlier, he would have been too upset and insisted I stay home. So I had kept silent. "I can put up with all of those symptoms as long as my legs are okay. My legs are the part of me that has to do the walking." Luckily, they weren't affected this time.

The day before the trek proved to be the most nerve-racking of all. The same "electrical" sensation was still present as well as the pressure in my head. The pain between my shoulders was back, too. My hands continued to shake and my equilibrium had been affected. When I tried to focus on the words I wrote for my speech at the opening ceremony, my vision became distorted and the words blurred together.

I watched from our patio as the afternoon sun slipped behind the pine trees and out of sight. The most difficult event of my life was only hours away. There was nothing left to do but read my speech one last time before retiring. I had constructed it one piece at a time, whenever there were a few spare minutes. Without realizing it, I had eventually produced ten pages of what I wanted to say before Lori, Sharon and I embarked on our mission.

Tim came up behind me and put his arms around my waist. "Last minute jitters?"

I nodded. "It's not only the actual trek, but this speech. It's going to take about ten minutes for me to read this thing. I'm just worried that I'll bore everyone to sleep before we even get on our way."

Tim smiled. "I really don't think you have anything to worry about in that department," he said. "Look at the Elks' fund-raiser. You're going to be great tomorrow. I can feel it."

I had no desire for the trek to be about me or even Lori. It was porphyria I wanted people to remember when they watched Lori and me walk by. When the purple ribbons were pinned to their shirts, I wanted them to focus on the disease, not the messenger.

"I just hope people really will become educated because of our walk."

"They will, hon. They will. Now, come on up to bed. You're going to need all the rest you can get for the big day."

Chapter 18

A Day of Thunder, A Day of Lightning

It began at dawn with an unexpected change before we left on our carefully planned schedule. I partially opened my still tired eyes and peered out the bedroom window. Thick sheets of rain fell from the sky. In disbelief, I pulled the covers over my head. Tim rolled over to my side of the bed and clicked on the television with the remote. He quickly flipped to the Weather Channel to see what had happened to cause such a drastic change in the forecast.

"Looks like we're in for a rough day," he said worriedly, peeling the covers off me. "They're predicting an ice storm to hit before nightfall." The telephone rang, interrupting his conveyance of the weather report.

"Tammy? You up? It's Sharon."

"Tim was just telling me the forecast."

"Donald just called me a few minutes ago. We're going to have to move the location for the starting ceremony," she said.

"Move the location? We can't do that! Everybody is

expecting us to be at the radio station!"

"We don't have any other choice, Tammy. It's too late to find any tarps to put up so people won't get wet." She tried to convince me. "Donald said he was going down to open up the American Legion hall. I'll call WHSB and have them put a sign on the door telling people where we'll be."

I just couldn't believe this was happening! We had tracked the weather for days and there was never any mention of an ice storm headed our way. All the snow had long since melted and flowers were already beginning to blossom. It was spring, not the middle of February!

"All right, do whatever you have to do. I'll be down there as soon as I can."

"Don't worry! Everything is under control," Sharon said, sensing the anxiety in my voice. "And Tammy. . . ."

"What?"

"Bring an umbrella and your winter coat."

We should have scheduled the ceremonies at the American Legion Hall from the beginning, I told myself. It was warm, with plenty of seating for the audience.

I stepped from room to room waking up the children, attempting to dress myself at the same time. When I reached Lori's room, the door was cracked just enough for me to peek inside. She was so beautiful, laying there with her black kitten nuzzled underneath her arm. I hated to wake her up.

"Hey, sweetpea," I whispered to her. "Rise and shine!"

She rolled and stretched, and the kitten did, too. Then she took a look out the window. "Mom, it's pouring rain." She buried her head under her pillow. Suddenly she pulled it out. "I don't care," she said. "We're going."

"You'd better believe it. Dress warm and bring your

jacket." I helped her out of bed as she got her bearings. Though she didn't complain of the extreme dizziness I often felt when getting up, she was experiencing a loss of equilibrium.

In a short while we were ready and joined Tim in the car which he was warming up. While Tim drove to the Legion Hall, the windshield wipers whisked back and forth, rapidly pushing rain aside. He stopped at the signal light where I could see the hall in the distance.

"That's odd," I commented to Tim.

"What's that, hon?"

"Well, look. The parking lot is filling with cars." I wiped the steam from the windshield to make sure I wasn't seeing things that didn't exist. As we got closer, I saw that it was true. Cars were lined around the large white building. Sharon's vehicle was right in front of the door with the red safety light swirling around on top of it.

When I walked through the door, I saw people I did not recognize. Some were setting up television cameras, large speakers, and spotlights along the walls. Perhaps I had walked into the wrong building, or some other function, I thought.

"Here she is, everyone! The lady of the hour!" Donald came up and gave me a big hug. The crowd applauded my arrival.

"Who are all these people?" I asked him.

"Well, take your coat off and come with me." Grinning, he whispered, "I'll introduce you."

The strangers smiled at me and I smiled back. There were all age groups, young, old and in between. The men in the blue and white uniforms I took to be the officers of the

Legion. Each of them reached his hand out to me as I walked past. "We're so happy you decided to let us help out, Mrs. Evans," one tall white-haired man said to me. "It's a pleasure to be at your service!"

"Where's Sharon?" I asked Donald.

"She took my car to pick up the coffee and donuts. We decided to leave the relief vehicle out front so everyone would know we were here." Donald, who was our ardent supporter and a local politician, hung up my coat and led me over to a table where several people were gathered around. "Tammy, I'd like you to meet Judy Highlander."

"I'm pleased to meet you, Judy." I shook her hand. As I did, I noticed the scars on her arms, ones that looked so much like my own.

"Oh yes," she said. "I have it, too. When I heard about all the things you had been doing to fight this awful disease, I had to come here and meet you in person."

I was astonished. Judy was the first person outside my family that I had been exposed to, with porphyria. I hadn't prepared myself for such a meeting. "You'll have to forgive me, Judy. I wasn't expecting to meet someone else with the disease. I've felt so alone," I said, choking back tears.

Judy raised her semi-paralyzed arm and waved it slowly across the table. "Look around you, my dear. There are others who feel just as alone. Some have come a long distance to meet you."

I followed her trembling hand as she pointed to each one. Yes, I recognized them now. Dark glasses, faces smothered with rashes, nonfunctioning arms and legs. I was looking at mirror images of myself. They were there with their children and spouses, each of them looking towards me to offer them hope. As tears of both sorrow and joy dripped down my cheeks, I reached into my purse for the bag of purple ribbons. Walking towards my brothers and sisters, I pinned one to each lapel.

A man from the back of the room pushed his way through the others. "My name is Jerry." He reached out his pale, blistered hand. When I reached out to shake it, he stopped me. "No, please don't. It hurts too much. I just wanted to show you that there are others who are suffering. There are others who need your help more than me."

Their pain was almost too much for me to bear. I had learned to accept my own physical scars, but it was an entirely different matter to witness theirs. Unlike my mother's, their suffering was out in the open, demanding recognition. I would have a lot to learn from them. "Thank you for coming this morning. You'll never know how much this means to me," I said.

Judy kissed me lightly on the cheek as I pinned her ribbon on. "No, my sweet girl. You are the one who deserves the thanks," she whispered. "When you come home from your long journey, we will have a get-together and talk." I looked over at Donald who had been listening and wiping his own tears with a handkerchief.

The room was filling up quickly. Sharon had returned and was mingling with the crowd, passing out our association's pamphlets. Just minutes before the program was to begin, I was startled to catch a glimpse of my mother sneaking in the side entrance, taking a seat. I took a ribbon, handed the bag to Donald and went over to her.

"Thank you, Mom," I said, pinning the ribbon to her jacket. She held me close to her. It felt so good knowing she was there.

"Excuse me, everyone," Donald announced from the microphone. "Could those of you still walking around take your seats. It's time to get started." He waited a few minutes for everyone to settle in. I took my place in the front row with the other guest speakers. The crowd of people hushed in reverence as the color guard of war veterans and Boy Scouts filed in. "Please stand for the Pledge of Allegiance, followed by our national anthem."

Each of the guest speakers took their respective turns at the podium. The political leaders of our community went first. The newly elected mayor, Camille Nerkowski, gave a simple speech to start the ball rolling. I could tell by her nervous smile that she really didn't know what to say. "I'm so happy you invited me to be a part of all this." She hurried back to her seat.

Beverly Bodem was a friend of my mother's and our state representative. "For many years, I have been Tammy's mother's friend. In all that time, I never realized that she had a dreaded illness. I would like to stress the importance of recognizing diseases such as this, and doing our best to fight them."

An aide to Congressman Bart Stupak, Sue Addams, read his congratulatory letter. I knew there wasn't much, if anything, that a political figure such as Congressman Stupak could do to help me, but it was a comfort to know I had his support.

I glanced over the room and noticed people listening intently. I hoped they would be as attentive when I gave my speech.

When Donald introduced Dr. Tatum, I saw some sort of plaque in the doctor's hand. He kept it hidden behind his suit jacket as he spoke, telling everyone about the lengthy and expensive testing procedures for porphyria. At the end of his speech, he called me to his side and revealed what he had been hiding. "And now I'd like to present Tammy with a telegram from our governor, John Engler."

I had debated right up until the last minute whether or not to read my entire speech. I didn't want to take too long or bore anyone. Nevertheless, after listening to those that had gone before me, I felt I needed to say what I had written and, long or not, the people there needed to hear it.

Although I couldn't see individuals through my watery eyes and the bright spot lights, I hoped I had a captive audience. The pages of my speech rattled in my shaking hands as I began telling them about how I had learned I had porphyria. I moved through the speech fluidly, all my apprehension gone.

"Today, I stand before you a self-educated woman in the field of the porphyrias," I said and explained the disease. Then I got to the most significant part. "But, it wasn't until my own daughter became ill with the symptoms of this awful disease that I had the courage to stand up and fight. It was then I knew something had to be done! My child's life was being threatened. I had to find a way to make people pay attention to this killer. It was at that point that I decided on this walk to Wyatt Clinic. I wish I could walk the whole country, but as you probably realize, in my condition, I can't. The walk to Petoskey for me is like walking across America for the healthy and strong. It is symbolic. My husband gave the event a name, the Trek for Truth. And with that, our mission begins."

The room was eerily silent as I left the podium to take

my seat. I couldn't see anyone past the glare of the spotlight. The frightening sensation that everyone had left the room came over me. It seemed Sharon, my family and I were the only ones still there. Just as I made my way past the blinding lights, the crowd rose to their feet, applauding wildly. They were all crying, everyone one of them, even my mother. Through the day blindness caused by porphyria, I finally saw the support I had always craved. Stepping off the stage, I was stepping back into the fold of my fellow men and women.

Reporters wanted photos of me. I posed with the dignitaries as the cameras clicked and the reporters videotaped our comments. Out of the corner of my eye, I noticed one of them approaching my mother for an interview. Another headed in Lori's direction, shoving a tape recorder in her face. During the days that Sharon and I had been arranging for the media to cover the story, Lori had made it clear to me that she felt shy and didn't want to speak to the media. "All right, everyone!" I shouted over the crowd. "It's time to walk the first mile!" As soon as I said it, the reporters scattered, each of them running out a different exit for the perfect shot at our departure.

The midnight blue state police car waited on the shoulder of the road, its red bubble light swirling overhead.

The moment of reckoning had arrived. There was no turning back.

The rain continued to pour down, putting a shiny gloss on everything. It was a cold rain. I put on my winter coat and raised my umbrella, wondering when, or if, the bad weather was going to let up.

Most of those who had attended the morning ceremony

rushed to their vehicles for cover. I had planned for everyone to walk the first mile of the trek with me, but only a small faction remained, consisting of my family, our Boy Scout troop, and the guest speakers. They huddled together behind the relief vehicle, shielding their bodies against the increasing winds. Sharon beeped her horn three times to signal the trooper we were ready to proceed. As Lori and I joined hands and raised them above us, Sharon drove her car slowly out of the parking lot. The miniature parade followed, cheering with enthusiasm as we walked onto the road. The trooper pulled his car up behind us and turned on the siren. We were finally on our way!

After we had walked only a few hundred yards, the wind began to gust even harder. I closed up my umbrella so it wouldn't blow out of my hand.

"You're going to have one heck of a walk in this stuff!" Dr. Tatum said, running to catch up with me. "You might consider postponing things if it doesn't clear up."

I looked up at the black clouds in the sky, knowing it was only going to get worse. "We can't do that. It'll throw the whole trek off schedule."

Dr. Tatum frowned his disapproval of my stubbornness. "I just don't want you being brought to the emergency room in the middle of the night, and not know what to do for you."

"I appreciate your concern, but I'll be all right. Lori and I can always take a break in the relief vehicle if it gets too bad."

Behind me, I could hear the rhythmic cadence of the Boy Scouts singing marching songs as we trudged forward. Just ahead on the right was the Country Party Store, the finish line of the first mile. There my family would leave off. A twinge of fear and sadness tugged at me. It was going to be difficult to say goodbye to Tim and my children, porphyria had made me utterly dependent on them. I would miss them horribly. But even more pressing than my maternal yearning was my anxiety over what lay ahead of me.

Reuben clung to my side as we stood in the store parking lot saying our goodbyes. He was the one that would have the most difficult time with my absence. Since my last attack he'd become apprehensive about losing me. I felt guilty leaving him like this, knowing how lonesome he would be. Somehow, I had to find the words to give him comfort while I was away, words that would make him strong enough to get through these days.

"Hey, little buddy! How about a hug for your momma before I go?" Reuben wasted no time in wrapping his arms around me. "I want you to be a good boy while I'm gone. Daddy's going to need all the help he can get, so I'm going to be counting on you." I petted his rain-soaked hair with my hand.

"I want to go with you," he squeaked, his voice cracking. "I promise I won't be any trouble." Saying goodbye was going to be more difficult than I'd thought.

I knew that, although his intentions were good, he would never be able to endure the strenuous task that loomed ahead of us. "You know how when you make the sketches for your comic book, and you work really hard so they turn out just right?" I asked him.

"Yeah. I like each one to be perfect."

"Those sketches wouldn't be the same, you couldn't really call them your own if someone else helped you draw them. Could you?"

"I would never let someone else help me with a

sketch, Momma," he said, adamantly.

"Well, that's how it is with the trek, Reuben. Lori and I are the ones who have this bad disease and we have to be able to say we did it on our own. Do you understand?"

He nodded his head and gave me a smile. "Yup! I think I do! But is it okay if I still miss you while you're gone?"

We both laughed and squeezed each other tightly. "If you didn't, I'd be very disappointed!" Reuben really did understand. He was going to be just fine.

Dan and Johanna were only a year older than Reuben, but their personalities were better equipped for letting me go. With a quick kiss and a pat on the back, they were ready to spend a week with Dad.

"I'll give you a call tonight to see how you're doing," Tim embraced me. "I want you girls to be careful. Don't overdo it."

"If it gets really bad, we'll sit in the car for a while."

"Don't worry, Dad," Lori said. "I'll keep my eye on her."

He hugged us both, whispering in a broken voice, "I love you guys. Don't get sick on me, you two, you hear?"

Tim started toward the van with the children, all of them waving farewell.

Lori, Sharon and I watched as the vehicles pulled away and out of sight. Already it seemed kind of lonely with them gone. We stood there for a moment, mentally preparing for the twelve miles ahead of us. Wind and sleet pelted our faces. "Well, ladies, no time like the present!" I said. Lori and I started up the road with Sharon following close behind in the relief vehicle.

Despite my fears and the weather, the next six miles didn't seem that bad. My legs held out and my spirit was undaunted, though my pace was rather slow. For a while Lori had her own pace going, faster than my own. With her headphones on, she bounced in synch with the music. There weren't as many cars on the road as there would be normally. The approaching storm was keeping people home. The few that did pass honked their horns when they saw the red flashing light on Sharon's car and our purple sweatshirts. Each time, I waved to the vehicles, thanking them for their gesture of kindness.

"Lori!" I called up to her. She couldn't hear a word I said with her music blaring so loud. "Lori! Come over here a minute!"

She turned around and slipped the headphones onto her shoulders. "Did you just say something to me, Mom?"

"Yes, dear. Would you please come back here. I want to talk to you." Instead of walking back to me she stood still in one spot and waited for me to catch up to her. "Lori, did you happen to notice the cars that have been passing by and beeping at us?"

"No, I guess I wasn't paying that much attention. Why?"

"They've been beeping their horns in support of what we're doing, Lori. Please wave back to them."

She gave me the typical "I didn't know" look. "I'm going to feel really stupid waving at people I've never seen before Mom!"

It was kind of ironic. Here we were, purposely walking down a country highway in the midst of an ice storm, and she was worried about how she'd feel about waving to strangers. "Lori, we already look pretty stupid out here. Waving back to people who are kind enough to show us they care isn't going to make us look dumber."

"Okay, sure. Why not." She turned back around and put her headphones back on.

I looked around. I had never been in a situation like this before either, but I wanted us to make friends along the way, not for myself, but for the fight against porphyria. The more people we touched and educated, the better.

By mid afternoon, we reached the parking lot of the Little Town Lounge, where I had planned to spend no more than half an hour to rest. It wasn't until we got inside that I realized how cold and wet we were. Lori was soaked to the bone, all of her clothes dripping with water. Mine were just as bad. Sitting down at the table, I began to feel a tightness building in my leg muscles that wasn't apparent while I was walking. The muscles cramped into hard lumps underneath the damp icy sheet of my skin.

"Not as easy as you thought it would be, eh, Tam?" Sharon pulled the boots from my burning feet. They felt like they were on fire, and looked swollen.

"I guess I didn't realize how tough it would be even though Lori and I trained for this walk between attacks. Still, I wouldn't care if it were four times as tough. We're not quitting."

Sharon nodded.

There were only a few patrons in the dimly lit tavern. A young biker couple, whose long brown hair made them look like twins, was sitting at the bar watching television, and at another table a balding trucker, with a red-checked shirt, was eating his lunch and looking at a map.

"What can I get for you gals?" The waitress put cocktail napkins down in front of us.

"Actually, I think we'll have something warm to eat. What kind of food do you serve?" I asked her.

"Everyone says our pizza is pretty good. I can have one ready in about ten minutes for you."

A hot bowl of soup would have sounded more appealing, but judging from her expression that was out of the question. We were in a bar, and we would have to eat what they served.

Lori and I changed into dry clothes in the bathroom. When we came out, Sharon was sitting with the truck driver.

"No!" she shouted. "You don't understand." She looked frustrated. "I said *trek*. You know, walking?" Sharon wiggled her fingers on the counter in front of him to signify what she meant. The trucker looked as though he couldn't understand a word she was saying.

After a few more minutes of trying to explain herself, Sharon gave up and just pinned a purple ribbon to his Carhat vest. "The only thing I got out of him was that he's from Quebec," she said with a laugh. "Do you know how hard it is to explain Trek for Truth to someone who doesn't speak English?" So, our first person-to-person opportunity to educate someone about porphyria was a man who only spoke French. We laughed all the way through our meal, thinking it could only happen to us. Secretly, I wondered if the rest of our teaching experiences were going to be just as difficult.

Putting my shoes back on was the most excruciating part of getting ready to walk the next six miles. Lori didn't seem to be in as much discomfort as I was and for a moment I felt jealous. I wanted to be young and resilient like she was. It would have made this journey a lot easier.

Getting up, Lori and I approached the young couple sitting at the bar. "Excuse me," I said, my voice a little shaky. I felt so odd walking up to a strange couple in a restaurant. "My daughter and I have a disease called porphyria. You may have heard of "the Vampire Disease"?...well, this is it. We're walking to Petoskey to promote awareness of it. Would you like to see one of our pamphlets?"

"We're not a damn bit interested in your problems, we've got our own," one "twin" said. The other piped in "damned right."

"And 'vampire' is apt," the woman cut in again. "You two definitely look spooky or out of this world or something." Their laughter resounded through the room.

Lori began crying. I stood there mortified.

Then, with my head down, I clasped Lori's hand and began to walk back to Sharon with her.

Halfway there, I stopped. I clenched my fists. No, I thought, I won't run away. That is what I've always done when people poked fun at the way I looked because of the disease. I'm not going to do that ever again.

"Lori, we're not running any more. Come on!"

The couple was surprised to see us back at their table again.

"Now what, freak?" the woman asked. "Looking for blood to drink?" she sneered. She and her partner cracked up.

"Hardly," I said, mustering as much courage as possible, "and if I was, you two would definitely not be choice meat."

Her eyes opened wide. I quickly dropped the insults and became serious. "I think you two crack so many bad jokes because you're afraid."

"Afraid of what? Vampires?" the man in the leather vest said defiantly.

"That something like porphyria could happen to you some day. It's like holding your breath when you pass cemeteries or looking away from those you consider freaks. Well, we're not freaks you know and our dreaded disease could happen to you or someone you love."

They both were silent now. "I'm going to leave this material so you won't be frightened anymore and will know the truth. That's the best way to deal with fears and no one knows that better than me."

I put my arm around Lori's shoulder and we walked toward Sharon who was still talking to the grizzled man who'd yelled to us.

When I looked over at the table where the young couple was, they were walking out. Clutched in the woman's hand was our pamphlet.

Suddenly, a gruff, rattly voice projected from a dark corner at the end of the bar. "Hey, ladies! Let us see one of those papers!" In the shadows, I noticed a seventyish man and woman nursing half empty glasses of beer. They had been there the whole time.

"I'll bring one over to you." I responded quickly. Grabbing Lori's arm, I propelled her in their direction.

"I heard about this walk on the radio this morning," the man said. "Now, what's that disease called again? I never heard of it before." He took a few minutes to look over the papers.

"Well, I just think it's so courageous what you and your daughter are doing," his wife commented. "Especially in this weather. Hank, give her a donation!" The man reached into his pocket, still reading the pamphlet.

"Thank you, but we're not asking for donations. We just want people to know a little more about this disease."

"Nonsense!" He slapped money into my hand. "If you have the guts to do something like this, the least we can do is help pay for your lunch."

We talked a little while longer. I thanked them for the donation and they thanked me for the education. Sharon came back around the bar and handed me another ten-dollar bill. "This is from the man in the other corner. He wouldn't take no for an answer."

I looked over at him and he pointed to the ribbon Sharon had pinned on his flannel shirt and gave me a little wave. I felt so guilty taking their money. Sharon and I had fully intended on paying for our own food wherever it wasn't donated by restaurants along the way.

"Well, look at that!" The waitress chipped in another dollar. "It's just enough!" She took the bill for our food from my hand. "You be careful out there," she added. "We'll be thinking about you!"

We headed toward the door, feeling good. "Hey, little girl!" the gruff voice bellowed again. Sharon turned around toward the man. "I hope your friend gets better real soon." Just as in the Elks Lodge, we were finding that people from all walks of life had a way of understanding once someone speaks out. I was beginning to have faith that one by one, I could turn cruel attitudes around.

As we walked out into the parking lot, there wasn't a soul in sight, no one to welcome the worn and weary. The excitement of our lunch had worn away. Though I felt weak in my stomach and my legs were bothering me again, it was time to begin walking again.

By the time we finished the day I was just grateful that Lori and I had made it that far. The only thing I wanted to do after eating was to take a hot bath and go to sleep, but an attack in the night would disrupt my plans.

Chapter 19

My Lonely Adventure

Sharon swung the car into reverse and revved the engine. Still the tires would not budge from their ice-caked craters. "Hang on!" she yelled to me. "I'll put it in drive and you can push!"

I maneuvered myself carefully on the slippery surface, looking for a rock or something sticking up out of the ground to secure my footing. Sharon put the car in gear and raced the engine again. I pushed as hard as I could without falling, but it was no use. The tires were glued in place.

"It's not going to budge!" I called out to her over the noise of the motor. "We'll just have to wait until it warms up a little bit!"

Sharon looked at me like I had lost my mind. The sleet was still coming down, putting another coating of ice on the one that was already there. The radio station said it was going to continue until nightfall. After that, it was going to change over to snow.

"Just go inside and get your shower!" She was becoming exasperated. "I'll keep rocking it back and forth till it breaks loose!"

I hobbled back inside and sat down on the edge of the bathtub, feeling totally useless. Even though the drastic change in the weather wasn't my fault, I felt responsible for what was taking place. If only I had waited another month to go on the trek!

The cool spray of water felt so refreshing on my burning skin. The boils on my back and arms had erupted into broken, oozing lesions. Since the night that Tim touched my back and discovered that they were there, I had done my best to hide them under long- sleeved sweatshirts. My feet hurt, too, much more than they had when I had gone to bed the night before. Tiny, pimplelike blisters were developing on each of my toes and a huge bubbly one appeared on my left heel. I lathered my body and rinsed under clear water. I was nearly finished, patting myself dry, when Sharon burst through the bathroom door.

"Tammy, I got the car. . . ." Her eyes opened wide in horror at the sight of me. "Oh my God!" I had never allowed her to see the gruesome sight that lay beneath my shirt.

I threw the towel up around my shoulders and grabbed on her arm. "Now you listen to me, Sharon Bruce! You're not going to utter one word about this to anyone! Do you hear me?"

"But, Tammy!" she stuttered. "I had no idea it was this bad. You can't go on in that condition!"

I turned away from her in my stubbornness and began dusting my body with medicated powder. "Oh yes, I can!" I defied her. "And you're not going to say a word! Besides, it's not as bad as it could be. It's been worse."

"Worse than this?" She reached for my arm.

"In a few days they'll be nothing but scars." I pushed

her hand back. "You won't even remember they were there. Please, Sharon, promise you won't say anything about it."

She nodded in silence at my request. She looked like she wanted to say or do something to make them heal faster, but we both knew that was impossible. "I just want to ask you one question, and then I'll never bring it up again."

"What's that?"

"Is it always like that? I mean, does it hurt bad all the time?"

I slipped my trek sweatshirt on over my head and turned to her. "It's only when I get an attack that they get like this. It hurts, but I guess I've gotten use to it." I reassured her. "Why don't you and Lori finish packing the car. I'll be along shortly and we can go get some breakfast." I took out my other slightly larger hiking shoes and began to put them on.

"Whatever you want." She was still in shock at what she had seen.

"And Sharon?"

"Yes?"

"Put a smile on your face and forget all about this, okay?"

"I can pretend it isn't there, if that's what you want," she said. "But I will never forget." She hurried out of the bathroom and called for Lori to help her.

"Dad just called," I heard Lori yell back. "I let him know we were all right. He said he'll come out to Hillman tonight to see us."

It took nearly half an hour of slip-sliding down the road to get there. Cramer's Restaurant was packed with people having their breakfast when we finally arrived.

"That's her, Fred!" The portly, middle-aged woman at the first table nudged her husband's arm. He looked up from the newspaper at me. "Well, I'll be! It *is* her!" They both stared intently as we took our seats at the table next to them.

"Good morning," I said to them, trying to be polite.

"Are you that nutty lady in the newspaper?" the woman asked in a loud voice. The rudeness of her remark caught me unawares.

"I don't know. I haven't seen this morning's paper yet." I extended my hand. "May I?"

The woman handed me her copy. "You made the front page. In fact, you made the *whole* front page! It's as if there's no *real* news."

Hearing her loud words, people in the crowded restaurant whispered back and forth to each other while staring at me. I kept my eyes on the paper. A color photo of those who had walked the first mile spread across the top of the paper. The headline in bold black letters read "TREK FOR TRUTH! EVANS'S JOURNEY BEGINS!"

The reporter had interviewed my mother. "We look healthy," Mom had said. "But when we have an attack, we look like death warmed over. What keeps me going is to push away the disease when I'm not having an attack. The toughest, scariest part of a prolonged attack is wondering if I'll ever come out of it. There's nothing my family can do but watch and pray."

I gave the paper back to the woman. I was glad that Mom had finally expressed herself about porphyria.

"Would you like to wear one of our purple ribbons?" Sharon asked the woman.

"Absolutely not," she said. "And that goes for Fred

too. We don't support nutty causes, especially weird looking people representing them."

"I'm sorry about your feeling that way," I said thinking that had this been only a few months ago, I'd have run home and hidden. "Meeting people and telling them about porphyria, our disease is why we're doing this."

Our meal had arrived and was getting cold, but I didn't care. I wanted to tell every person I could about our mission even those who refused to listen. Sharon caught my attention before I went off to talk to anyone else. "Sit down and eat," she commanded. "You can handle these detractors better on a full stomach."

"Maybe, maybe not," I snapped back "It all depends on whether they make me feel sick"

"Yes, Mother." She grinned at me sheepishly.

"You can joke all you want, but someone has to keep an eye on you!"

I ate my breakfast and, in turn, made Lori eat hers. As soon as we were done, we went from table to table and pinned more purple ribbons on the people who were around and asked everyone to sign our sweatshirts. I nearly forgot about my aching feet that were crammed into my hiking boots. I knew that as soon as it was time to go, Lori and I would be all alone again for the long walk to Hillman. That made it hard to say goodbye.

But we needed to move forward. After loading our jacket pockets with candy bars, Sharon, Lori and I headed out. Although the pavement was tremendously slick, the shoulder of the road wasn't too bad for walking. The pebbles underneath the ice provided just enough grip to our shoes so we wouldn't fall. It was the force of the wind in our faces that provided the biggest challenge. Large pellets of hail flew into our eyes and pelted our skin, making it difficult to see where we were going. Nevertheless, Lori put her headphones on, and away she went.

I walked a bit slower, really feeling the stiffness from the previous day's walk. The blisters on my toes rubbed against the inside of my boot with each step. I thought about how awful it must have been for Sharon to see what porphyria really did to me, the painful rash it always left behind as a sign of its existence. She had witnessed the excruciating stomach cramps and the relentless nausea, but not the problems with my skin until this morning. The sores, this time, had moved from my face to my torso. In a way, I was glad. If I had to endure them, at least they were hidden from sight most of the time.

I had been spending so much time and effort putting the trek together and fighting porphyria as a whole that I had been neglecting caring for the symptoms that plagued me. I didn't want to think of that now. I put on my headphones and filled my mind with music.

"Tammy!" Sharon pulled the car up beside me. "It's time to take a break. You're limping, badly."

I looked down and noticed she was right. The pain from the blister on my heel suddenly felt agonizing. My foot seemed to have swollen to twice its normal size inside my shoe. Lori was quite a distance up the road, sitting on a large rock waiting for us. Sharon drove up ahead and Lori got in the car.

"How far have we gone?" I took Lori's place on the rock and started untying my boot.

"About five miles," Sharon answered.

"What were you doing back there, Mom? It looked like you were in a trance."

"Nothing, really. Just thinking." I loosened the laces and slowly slipped out my foot. When I peeled my sock back, an even larger watery bubble appeared. "Lori, get the first aid kit out of the back seat. I'm going to put some mole skin on this."

She got out of the car and handed me the box. "Dad says you're supposed to put mole skin on *before* it looks that bad, not after."

"I don't really see how I have much choice, Lori." I cut a strip out of the square of soft padding. "The damage has already been done, and we still have six miles to go."

Our hats and jackets were covered with the same thin sheet of ice that blanketed the road. The sleet was turning into light rain mixed with snow. As far as I remembered, not a single vehicle had passed by us. "Since we've stopped, we may as well eat some lunch." I climbed into the car with them. "What kind of goodies do we have?" Lori pulled out a sack of sandwiches she made before we left and showed us a box of donuts. Sharon stepped out for a leisurely stretch while we put together our little roadside picnic.

"You know," Lori said, chewing on her sandwich, "I felt pretty good during that last five miles. My legs aren't tired at all. How about you?"

"While I was walking my legs worked fine and without any pain. Now that we are resting, not so great." I could feel the muscles knotting up in my calves. My feet felt like they were on fire. "But not bad, I guess. A little stiff perhaps," I lied to her.

We ate our lunch and laced our boots back up. My feet were so swollen that I had barely enough shoestring to tie them. The hardest part was starting to walk again. I could tell that the next six miles were going to be pure torture.

We waited until our allotted half hour was up. Mike had told us that, it was better either to take ten-minute breaks, or to wait longer than thirty minutes to start up again. I didn't really understand why. It had something to do with body chemicals. Since he was the hiking expert, I figured it would be wise to follow his instruction. I latched on my headphones and selected one of my tapes before we headed out. Then we began walking, moving toward our destination.

Lori stayed by my side for the second part of the day, walking slower than she normally would. I think she was feeling sorry for me as I limped along. "What are you listening to?" she asked.

"What?"

"I said," she pulled the earphone from my head, "what are you listening to?" She took my headphones off and held them up to her ears to sample my music. "I can't believe it!" She laughed hysterically. "You're listening to marching music!" Lori grabbed my tape recorder and ran back to the car. I could hear them behind me, roaring over my choice of listening pleasure.

"I like that music!" I stated emphatically as she handed the recorder back. Still laughing. I put the earphones back on and turned the sound up louder. In a strange way, it really was helping me keep going.

We trudged along in the mist that was quickly turning to thick white flakes of snow. I still could not believe the weather. In all my years of living in northern Michigan, I had

never seen anything like it in April. My back hurt and feet
continued to ache, swelling and burning in the toes and heels.

"Have you noticed that not one single car has passed
us lately?" I asked Lori.

"There were a couple before we stopped for lunch.
Didn't you see them? I waved, just like you told me to."

I hadn't seen them. "No. I guess I didn't notice."

"But you're right. I haven't seen any since. You'd
think that everyone would be out and about with the break in
the weather," she said.

I wouldn't have referred to it as a break per se.
However, the lightly falling snow was much better than the
blinding sleet. "Strange!" I laughed. "Maybe they all know
something we don't."

I stumbled along, trying to quicken my pace. I didn't
want to hold Lori back any more than was necessary. With
every single step, I prayed that we would see the Thunderbay
Resort towards which we were heading in the near distance
soon. I was hurting badly and I was so tired. It was only the
second day, and I was afraid that if I had a serious attack I
would have to stop.

"Just another mile or so, Mom." Lori said. She could
tell how tired I was. "I'm sure it's just around the bend.
Maybe you should eat one of your candy bars. I'll run back
to the car and get you a bottle of juice." Before I could stop
her, she was gone.

I hadn't been paying very close attention to my sugar
intake. When I was making the preparations for the trek, I
had upped my carbohydrate intake and planned that on the
trip I would adopt one that would counterbalance the amount
of energy I would be expending. Somewhere in the turmoil,

I had completely abandoned my plan, and now I was paying the price.

The candy bar was half gone when she returned. "Here, Mom." Lori handed me the juice. "I put the straw in it for you already."

"Thanks." Ever since my last porphyria attack I had to drink all of my beverages through a straw. When the paralysis had struck, it had taken away my ability to swallow correctly. After many weeks, I learned how to drink all over again, but when I was tired I still needed the assistance of a straw so I wouldn't choke.

I drank the juice down as quickly as I could. Within minutes, I was thinking clearer and feeling better, we were able to continue on.

"Better, now?" Lori asked.

"Yes, much!"

Lori raised her hand and pointed down the road to a stand of majestic maple trees surrounded by the lush green grass of a golf course. "Look, Mom! We're almost there!" She took my hand and clasped it in her own. Together, we walked the last hundred yards to the large wooden sign that read "THUNDERBAY RESORT." It looked luxurious almost at that moment like a mirage. Unfortunately, I had to look quickly away: the bright sunlight sizzled my skin.

Feathery wisps of steam rose up from the bath water. I slid my body into it slowly, melting away the clammy dampness of my skin. The sores on my back stung with pain as I lowered myself into the water, but it didn't matter. Even as my skin burned, the rest of my aching body craved the therapeutic heat of the indoors.

I had plenty of time to lie there and relax in the tub.

Lori and Sharon would be keeping themselves busy playing with all the gadgets and enjoying the spaciousness of our deluxe suite. It was a gorgeous resort. All of the buildings were handcrafted log lodges with spacious balconies for viewing the scenery. Towering Jack pines framed the perimeter of the golf course that could be seen from the bay window in our room. Just outside our door stood a miniature log gazebo that housed a whirlpool tub and sauna. As the only guests at the resort, we enjoyed unlimited privacy.

I sank deeper into the soothing water and laid the damp washcloth over my face. The tension of the last eleven miles, all drifted away into the steamy clouds. I let go all of the pain, frustration and worry and began to relax.

"Mom!" I vaguely heard the sound of my daughter's voice. Thump, thump, thump! "Mom, are you still alive in there?"

Lori's incessant pounding on the door forced me out of the now icy water. "What?" I answered half asleep. "What do you want?"

"You've been in there for hours!" she chastised me. "Mrs. Bruce and I are starving! Hurry up so we can go get something to eat!"

My body was heavy and wobbly from the long nap. I hurried as fast as I could to wrap a towel around myself and open the door. "I'll be ready in just a few minutes."

"You were asleep in the bathtub, weren't you?"

"No, not at all. Just relaxing."

"You were so asleep!" She laughed heartily. "I could hear you snoring!"

My face flushed in embarrassment. Sharon called out from the other room. "Just think, Lori. If your mother had drowned in there, we could go home!" They both had a moment of entertainment at my expense.

Carter's Sub Shop was one of the restaurants along our trek that had agreed to donate a meal. "My boss said you could have your choice of anything from the menu. Go ahead! Eat as much as you want!" The teenage girl behind the counter seemed glad to have us for her lone customers on the stormy night. We accepted her offer to feast on the luscious foot-long sandwiches.

I couldn't enjoy them though, as I sat there leaning against the back of the chair, I felt the blisters on my back growing more and more painful. Fluid oozed from the sores, soaking the back of my shirt. Whatever medication I had, adequate or not, needed to be applied so I could get some relief. Excusing myself, I left.

I lay flat on my stomach across the double bed, my arms wrapped securely around the pillow. Sharon smoothed the medication on my back, "Did that hurt?"

"No. It was just cold. Let me lie here while that stuff dries."

"Alright, Tammy, but I'll be back to check on you."

Ten minutes later, Sharon returned to find me still lying on my stomach watching television.

"Okay?" She asked.

"Sharon, this is part of my disease. I know how horrible it must look to an outsider, even a friend, but I have to live with this and get on."

"I'm sorry, but I don't like to see you in pain, any kind of pain." Her eyes welled up with tears.

Sharon had a gentle spirit, and a very loving heart. It

was the quality I admired most about her. I held my hand out to her and she took hold of it. "It's fine now." I gave her a squeeze. "Everything's going to be just fine."

Lori stayed in her own room the entire evening, calling her friends and telling them about the trek. "Hold the phone calls to a few minutes, hon. We're going to get charged for them." Just as we had settled in for the night and began writing in our journals, a knock came at the door. It was Tim.

"Hey, there's my favorite girl!" He came to my side and kissed me gently. "How are you holding up?" Seeing my back he looked concerned. "Bad dear?"

"It'll be fine by morning." I turned on my stomach so he couldn't see how bad it really was.

"How are the kids? Do they miss me yet?"

Tim reached into his pocket and pulled out a huge stack of cards and hand drawn pictures. "Oh, I'd say they miss you, all right. They wanted to come with me, but the roads are getting really bad. I didn't want to risk getting stuck out there with them along."

"You will tell them how much I love and miss them?" My heart was breaking being away from my children.

"Of course I will. They wanted me to pass along the same to you. I brought you more mole skin. I figured your feet would need it about now, but I didn't anticipate your back."

"Oh, thank you!" I took it from his hands. The soft spongy pads had become worth their weight in gold. "I can take pain from one source, but when they all combine, I'm in trouble," I grinned.

Tim went into Lori's room and visited for a few minutes with her. Then he came back and he and I talked for a while longer. I told him all about the wonderful caring people we had met along our journey, as well as the not so caring ones. Sharon joined in the conversation, remembering her promise. She never uttered a word as to how badly I was feeling. Tim left, thinking that everything was running smoothly.

"Thank you, Sharon."

"You're welcome," she replied softly, crawling into her bed. Without another word, she turned off her lamp and went to sleep.

I stared out the window at the blowing and drifting snow, wondering what it would be like the next morning. Darkness surrounded me. All my emotions flooded together. The tantalizing thoughts of cheering crowds and news cameras faded out of existence. My loving husband and children were miles away, replaced only by the reality of my weakening body.

Chapter 20

Opportunities

Waves of gurgling nausea woke me from my fitful sleep. As I rolled on my side to inhibit the painful cramping in my stomach, the scabbed sores on my back rubbed against the stiff bed sheet. During the night they had broken open, their burning poison oozing forth. Yesterday's fear of walking because of painful feet had been replaced by a greater fear, that of my real worst enemy, the all-out porphyria attack....

With a flick of the remote, I tuned to the local forecast to see what weather problem could also hamper my progress. The announcer had a saccharin voice. "A pleasant change has finally come our way. Today we'll see clear skies and bright sunshine, with a high in the low seventies."

I had hoped for some relief from the brutal winds and icy spray of sleet and snow. Lingering clouds and a cool breeze were what I had envisioned. But the sun was out and it was burning bright. For most people a sunny day is sheer joy, but I was not as lucky. This was the kind of forecast I feared most, the one I had hoped would not reveal itself until

241

Lori and I finished the trek and were safely indoors
again. It was not to be. I would have to take extra care
today to shield my body from the burning rays, and
press on with my mission. If not careful, I would cook
out there like an egg in a frying pan.

Carefully dressing so as much skin was covered as
possible, I remembered to put on my dark glasses, the ones
that Tim had ordered especially for days such as this. I
didn't want to scare Sharon and Lori so I adopted an
upbeat manner. "Come on, girls! Time to rise and shine!"
I opened the drapes.

Sharon shielded her eyes from the light and rolled
toward the wall. "You are a cruel and vicious woman,
Tammy Evans!"

"I know, but that's what you love most about me." I
hobbled into Lori's room and proceeded to wake her. She
gave nothing but a muffled groan in return.

"You're in a hyper mood." Sharon called.

"I feel pretty good today," I lied, desperate to go on.

Only a short while later back on the highway I saw
that M-32 was bringing us deeper into the heart of the state.
Rolling hills of birch, maple and pine trees lined the two-lane
road. The beautiful secluded area was well known as prime
hunting ground for deer and elk; our next stop, Atlanta, was
even nicknamed "The Elk Capital of the World." There
weren't many permanent, year-round residents in this area,
mainly closed-up hunting camps and vacation homes dotted
the landscape. As the snow melted under the strength of the
warm sunshine, the clean fragrance of spring reappeared in
the air. Although I would have loved to feel the sun on my
skin, I made sure my arms were completely covered by my

sweatshirt, and the visor of my hat was pulled down to shield my face. Lori also covered up. She stood next to me. We began another day of our journey.

I reached into my pocket to find my cassette tape so that I would have music for company. There, I touched the plastic bag that contained the purple ribbons. There were lots of them in there. Shiny purple strips of acetate, the symbol of our cause. Hopefully, there will be some people waiting for me at the other end of this trail who would take some home.

Sharon hadn't said much to me before we got on our way earlier that morning. I wondered if it was because I'd asked her to keep my secret. I felt badly, too, because I was angry with myself for doing the same thing that Mother had done to me for so many years, the thing I'd promised I would never do: Cover up. Now I realized that in that brief moment with Sharon I had allowed myself to be part of hiding the truth. It was my self-appointed mission to bring porphyria from the dark places in which it hid, into the light. Ugly or not, the world had to be informed of its existence and danger.

We stopped for lunch under the shade of some maple trees. It felt so good to kick off my shoes and let my feet breathe in the fresh air. Lori looked bushed from the heat and from being swaddled in heavy clothing. Even though Lori had not yet displayed the profound sensitivity to sunlight that I had, I knew this complication could come anytime. She'd kept her sweatshirt and hat on, as I instructed, to shield her body from the dangerous rays.

"How far do you think we've gone today?" Lori asked.

I fumbled around for the notebook that contained the

odometer readings. "Well, we've probably walked a little more than halfway, maybe a little farther. I'd say close to ten miles already." Lori looked amazed.

"If we keep up the same pace, we should reach Rosie's Cafe just in time for an early supper," I added.

We packed up the remains of our lunch and attended to our primitive bathroom duties. I couldn't help noticing that Lori was moving slowly and acting lethargic.

"How are you doing?" I asked her.

"I'm okay. It's just that I tire much more easily than I ever have. Do you think it's our disease?" I didn't know whether to smile or cry at her mention of our awful bond. "Sometimes I feel like I'm going to nod right off," she continued.

"Want some of my 'marching music'? It might help keep you awake!" I grinned.

"No, thank you. I'd rather nod off than march to your tunes!"

We both laughed.

"Just think, Lori. In another ten miles, three and a half hours, you'll be sitting down to the most scrumptious Italian food in the world." I tried to give her something to look forward to.

"Rosie's Cafe in Atlanta sounds like the best food ever, from what I hear!" Sharon chimed in.

Later that afternoon when we finally tramped through the door at Rosie's Cafe, it was like waking up in Italy. The restaurant was owned by Jenny and Mike Bergelli who had moved to the tiny village of Atlanta to get away from the hustle and bustle of Detroit. Only a year ago, they purchased an old rundown building at the entrance to the town. They and their children fixed it up and opened the little Italian restaurant. Tim had lunch there often and told me it was delicious.

Greeting us warmly, Jenny and Mike made us feel at home in their tiny establishment, showing us to a beautiful, candlelit table.

"We're so happy you're finally here!" Mike hugged us all. "I've prepared a marvelous feast for my weary travelers." He practically bounced up and down around us, he was so full of excitement at our arrival. "How about we start you off with a nice hot bowl of minestrone soup?" He bustled to the kitchen to get it ready for us.

"I have to congratulate you," I said to Lori. "You walked eighteen miles today, and without a single word of complaint!"

"I'm going to complain now, if that's all right with you. My legs feel like lead and my butt is going to fall off my backside any minute now!" It was hard for me to put Lori through the walking, but without the trek there seemed to be no hope for our family. I was going to make sure that by walking now, she would have many walking days ahead.

Jenny brought out large carafes of iced mineral water. "Here, this will help cool you off."

I hadn't paid much attention to what time it was. When I looked at my watch and found it was five o'clock, I was amazed at how quickly the day had passed.

Just as we settled in and began enjoying the homemade minestrone, two new customers entered the restaurant.

"Grandma!" Lori jumped up and hugged my mother, instantly forgetting about her aches and pains. "I'm so glad to see you!"

Mom looked over at Sharon. "She arranged it!"

Sharon, who was usually so boisterous, just smiled.

"We didn't think you would be here so early. Your father and I wanted to be here first and surprise you," Mom added.

"I really am glad you came." I hugged them both. "It really feels good to see you. It was kind of lonely."

Mom and Dad pulled up seats, ready to enjoy their supper with us. "The whole town is buzzing over the trek, Tammy. I keep getting phone calls from people asking how you're doing. Since I didn't really know, I figured I'd better come here and find out." Mom was filled with more excitement than I had seen in her in ages.

Jenny and Mike began bringing out plate after plate of delicious Italian delicacies until we just couldn't swallow another bite. "There!" Mike shouted, his hands raised in the air when we had finished, "you should feel all better now!"

I nodded. "Our stomachs are full, and the company is wonderful." We actually did feel better!

During our two-hour banquet, the restaurant filled up. Sharon and I went to work, walking through the room with our pamphlets and ribbons. Some people graciously took the pamphlet, but others motioned us away and only a few accepted the ribbons or asked any questions. I felt disappointed by the lack of enthusiasm. I didn't really know how to take their reactions, except perhaps that the unexpected interruption of their dinner hour had made them less than interested in our cause.

"I'd like a pamphlet!" a frail woman's voice called. I turned around to see where the voice was coming from.

In the back corner of the restaurant sat an old,

white-haired woman in a booth all by herself. She must have been eighty-five or ninety years old, but with a smile that lit up the room. "I'd sure like to put on one of your purple ribbons, too."

I walked towards her table. "I'll be rooting for you, girl!" she called out cheerily. I started to pin on a ribbon. "No, I'll do it; I like doing things myself."

Her name, she told me, was Isabel, and she pinned on the ribbon with trembling, aged fingers. Afterward, she reached in her change purse, pulled out a five-dollar bill and placed it in my hand. "Now, I don't want you to tell me you don't want this. I'll be terribly offended if you do. Somewhere down the road it will come in handy, so just put it in your pocket, and remember me as you go on your way."

"Thank you, Isabel," I accepted her kind gift, "You've just been a pleasure to talk to." I felt I had met a kindred spirit.

"There's just one more thing, dear, before you go. Could you pronounce the name of your disease for me? I want to get it right when I tell my friends."

"Yes, I'm curious about that, too." Another voice came out of the invigorated crowd, which had witnessed my encounter with Isabel. I turned to find a ruddy-faced man sitting directly behind me with a pencil and notepad in his hand.

"Are you a reporter?" I asked him.

"Name's Bill. Bill Huntly, *Monroe Tribune*," he said rather gruffly.

As I spelled porphyria and told him about the disease, I saw other people watching. "We would like to hear, too," another said, piping up. I described the symptoms and the fact that Lori was its newest victim. Then I told him about our Trek for Truth, what it symbolized, and our experiences so far. The reporter wrote it all down in his little notebook, never looking up, but others called us back to their tables and we ended up pinning on a lot of purple ribbons.

"Bill, you should get a picture of these girls to put in that paper of yours!" Mike yelled out to him from the kitchen. I gathered that they knew each other well.

The reporter smiled and replied, "Well, get yourself out here and I'll kill two birds with one stone. You could stand the publicity!"

Bill Huntly snapped his photos and thanked me for the interview. It wasn't the national coverage which porphyria needed, but I was grateful.

Then it was time to leave. I said goodbye to my parents, Jenny and Mike, Bill and Isabel, as well as our newfound friends. The long, lonesome day turned into a celebration of my cause. I rejoiced in the surprising way it had all turned around for us.

Inside our motel room, I called out, "First one in the tub" and hurried to undress. I sank deep into the therapeutic pulse of the whirlpool, allowing the jets of steaming water to pound at the stiffening muscles in my legs. In the bubbling waters, I let all of my worries and pain drift away, relaxing completely. When I got out, I passed Sharon and Lori, already asleep. Getting into bed, I felt really good about the evening: we *were* making a difference.

"Wake up, Mom! C'mon! I have to tell you the neatest thing!" Lori plopped the heavy, plastic grocery sack on top of my still sleeping body. "You'll never guess what just happened to me!"

I opened one eye to see the exuberant face of my first-born child. She started taking items out of the sack, placing them in front of my face.

"I went over to that gas station next door to the motel. Ya know which one I mean, Mom?"

"Uh huh."

"The guy behind the counter asked me if I was one of the walkers on the Trek for Truth and I told him 'yes.' He told me to pick out anything I wanted for our breakfast and it would be their donation to us."

"That's wonderful, honey." I still had only one eye open. "Did you remember to say thank you?"

"Yup! I did! And you know what else? Mom, are you listening to me?"

"Yes. I'm listening."

"He asked me all kinds of questions about porphyria, and I was able to answer every one of them!"

I sat up. "I really am proud of you, Lori. You did a good job of communicating what this trek is all about this morning." I hugged her.

"Does this mean I'm an acovate, now?" She looked at me with her twinkling blue eyes.

"That's *advocate*. And yes, Lori, you can call yourself that now." She made me smile. It was a beautiful way to begin another long day on the long road ahead.

A short while later, we were again on our way, hoping new friends would come upon us at each turn in the winding road. Lori and I walked together most of the day. We talked, not like mother and daughter, but like comrades would. I felt so close to her. I was beginning to know an aspect of her I had never recognized before. As we marked off the miles, I saw the young woman she was becoming rather than the child she used to be. It brought tears of joy to my eyes and worry for her future.

Our journey that day came to an end in the sparsely populated village of Vienna Corners. The name was apt. It had exactly two corners. On one stood the auto repair shop, owned by Vincent Brighton. Vincent was one of the contacts Donald Packard had set up for us. It was at his home that we were scheduled to spend the night.

Vincent's auto shop had a kind of "Mayberry R.F.D." air about it. Old calendars hung on the wall next to the price list for different automobile parts. A fiftiesh man wearing an orange hunting jacket sat in one of the two wooden chairs reading a magazine and smoking a pipe. He didn't even lift his head up when we walked in. Sitting in the other chair was a chestnut-haired, pleasant looking woman.

"You must be the walkers," she greeted us.

"I'm Tammy. This is my daughter, Lori, and my friend Sharon."

"I'm Vincent's wife, Candy. Vince just told me you were going to be spending the night at our house." She didn't look particularly happy at the thought.

I began feeling embarrassed about the situation when she added, "Vince does this kind of thing to me all the time. But don't you worry. We've got plenty of room and you'll be right comfortable. I'll be home late. I have to shoot pool tonight, so I won't be around to show you around or anything."

"Well, I suppose we could go and get some supper. We could use some time to relax and unwind. Where would be a good place to eat?"

She started to laugh. "The best place to eat would be

the only place to eat, that bar across the street there. That's it. And they only serve one thing. Pizza."

Vince came out of the back room, rubbing his hands on a rag. "Well, you made it. Good to see ya!" he beamed at us.

"Hey, you girls go on over to the Sport and have a pizza on me. I already told them you were coming. I'll be over as soon as I'm done here and I'll take you to our house."

We made a quick exit, feeling a little out of place. That feeling grew at our next stop.

The Sport Bar was a hopping version of your typical dive. As we entered the log and mortar building, I saw silver Mylar balloon fish and gilded fishnets hung from the ceiling, dangling over our heads. The people inside were just as unique. Two men with full beards, dressed in overalls and blue baseball caps, hovered over the pool table in the middle of the room. I looked down and saw that the table's change dispenser was lying on the floor. Nobody was making any money off that pool table! Another man with a shaved head, in his thirties, sat at a table in the far corner with two empty beer mugs and a half-full one in front of him. He was mumbling to himself. A white-haired man who looked to be in his eighties sat at the bar talking to the barmaid. She had bottle-blonde hair tied on top of her head.

"I know what you guys are thinking," I said as Sharon and Lori nudged me as if they wanted to leave immediately. "Let's just give this a chance and see where it leads us."

"Mom, I don't want to be disrespectful, but there's no way this can lead anywhere good. I'm not staying."

"Gaylord is only twenty miles up the road, Tammy," Sharon broke in. "We could drive there, spend the night at the Holiday Inn, and I could drive you back here in the morning to continue your walk."

"I'm disappointed in you. You aren't even willing to give Vienna Corners a chance. No. We're going to stay for a while and have a pizza. Vince was nice enough to pay for it so the least we can do is eat it."

Sharon started walking to the door.

"Where are you going?" I asked.

"Well, if you're going to make us stay here, I'm going to get the video camera. No one at home will ever believe what this place is like if I don't have documented evidence. I'm telling you right now, Tammy. If their house resembles this bar in the least little bit, I'm outta there," Sharon stated emphatically.

"All right. I'll go along with that. But let's just give it a chance before bailing out."

Vince finally arrived. We got in the car and Sharon followed his red Chevy truck down the dirt road that led to his home. To our surprise, it was quite charming inside. It had comfortable antique furniture and grandfather clocks in each room complete with lovely dried flower arrangements on the tables.

"Go ahead and make yourselves at home," Vince said. "There are two spare bedrooms down the hall, and the bathroom is right over there." He pointed to our left.

"I really appreciate your putting us up like this, Vince. You have a lovely home."

"Well, thanks. Say, I'm sorry about the mix-up with my wife. That was all my fault. Sometimes I just get so busy I forget to tell her things."

"I understand." I didn't really, but he was so kind and hospitable that I couldn't say anything else.

We said goodnight to our host. Sharon and I gave Lori one of the bedrooms to herself and she fell asleep almost immediately. Sharon and I shared the other. After changing into our nightclothes and settling in, I surveyed the damage to my skin in the mirror.

"Look, Sharon. It's not as bad as I thought it would be."

"What about those red bumps and the nasty trail of white pustules on your arms?"

"I guess there's just no way to avoid them. I really covered up."

"Maybe some more ointment will help."

"I hope so."

"You have a big day ahead of you tomorrow. You have to take care of yourself or you won't be able to help anyone else."

"You're a good friend, Sharon."

She laughed, remembering all we had been through together in the past few days. "You can say that again!"

Chapter 21

Storms

"Momma!" Lori cried out to me from the bedroom across the hall the next morning. I knew it had to be something serious if she was calling me "Momma." I opened the door to find her curled up on the side of the bed. One arm was flung over her eyes and the other pressed against her stomach.

"Momma, I don't feel so good. My head and back hurt and I feel like I'm going to throw up." Her face was extremely pale and her eyes, when she took her arm away, were tearing and had dark circles under them.

I felt her forehead to see if she might have a fever. Perhaps, I told myself, trying not to think of our dreaded affliction, she was coming down with a cold or a virus. The bone-chilling rain we had walked in certainly hadn't helped.

"You don't have a fever, honey." I was slightly surprised. "Do you think it may have been that pizza we ate last night? We all had it," I said, puzzled.

"I don't know," she moaned. "My body just hurts, Mom."

I rubbed her forehead and her tummy, just like my grandmother had done for me when I was little. For some reason it usually had a soothing effect, but it didn't seem to have one on Lori. I looked down to see my hands trembling. Suddenly I knew why. Lori didn't have the flu or any other common ailment. It was porphyria not only attacking me but my daughter also. I felt angry.

"I think it would be a good idea if you took a break from walking today. You can lay down in the back seat of the car and rest. How does that sound?"

"But you'll be all alone," Lori worried.

"I'd much rather walk alone than have you get sicker. Besides, I have my music to keep me company. Remember?"

Lori cracked a smile. "So that's what you call it."

Sharon and I loaded the car while Lori slowly dressed herself. When we took our bags out to the car, I noticed the rain had turned to snow overnight. It was a slushy, icy snow, turning the ground into a muddy mixture that stuck to our shoes. In the sky to the west, black storm clouds were beginning to form again. The wind suddenly picked up, blowing hard crystal pellets into our faces. It was going to be another challenging day.

The first mile or so my legs felt unusually heavy beneath me. They were like stiff beams of lead, requiring every ounce of my energy to move them. The highway was starting to weave in and out through the snow-covered terrain, each turn in the road becoming sharper than the one before. Five miles out of Gaylord, the hills would start. That was something I wasn't looking forward to. With thirteen miles to walk before the rugged terrain began, I had to concentrate on the immediate problems not the distant ones, I told myself.

I walked slowly for several hours, listening to a radio station instead of my tapes. The outside world seemed far away. It was as if I were on an entirely different planet than everyone else. My thoughts drifted toward my home and my other children as well as my husband. Looking at my watch, I imagined them getting ready for school and work. Dan would be pounding on the bathroom door, yelling at Johanna to finish getting dressed in her bedroom so he could take a shower. Reuben would be sitting at the breakfast table, intently studying the back of a cereal box while he ate. Tim would be telling everyone to hurry up, gulping his hot coffee from his mug while searching for a clean pair of socks to wear. Inevitably, the telephone would ring, one of the kids' friends arranging to meet him or her at the corner so they could walk to school together. The weekday mornings at our house were probably much the same as in any other. I hadn't given them much thought.

Now, as I trudged along at a snail's pace with the wind in my face, I wanted nothing more than to be back at home with my family, safe in the thick of their morning ritual.

I looked back at the car where Lori was sleeping, wondering if she was all right. She really hadn't looked well this morning. I knew she felt badly not being able to walk today. I felt sad not having her beside me, but no matter what, I knew I had to push on for Lori's sake and for my own.

Chapter 22

Miles to Go

It was day five. I didn't want to know what time it was. There were still fifteen more miles to go. The air had grown much colder. Rolling black clouds brought forth gustier winds that pushed against my body, making it difficult to keep a steady gait. More snow was falling. Within an hour, soft white snowflakes turned into hard pellets of ice again, whipping at me as I made my way out of the protection of the trees and into the open fields. The wind increased. An uneven layer of sleet had formed beneath the snow and my feet slipped with each step I took. I had to hold my arm up against the wind to keep the ice pellets from shooting into my eyes.

Suddenly, I heard Sharon calling my name.

"Tammy! Get in the car, Tammy!" Sharon pulled the car up beside me. "You can't walk in this stuff!"

"I have to keep going if we're going to make it to Gaylord on time," I yelled back.

"Look, get in the car and I'll drive you ahead a couple of miles," she insisted.

Now I was angry with her. Maybe the national media wasn't watching over my shoulder, but some people were counting on me to be honest in my effort. How could I ever look any of them in the eye, knowing I had cheated? "No! I won't do it!" I picked up my pace, walking a little faster.

"No one will know you shaved off a couple of miles!"

I stopped dead in my tracks and stomped towards the open window. I thrust my ice-covered head into the car, just inches from her face. She saw the rage burning inside of me and jolted back in her seat. "*I* will know, Sharon! And that's all that counts!" I smacked the side of the car with my fist and walked away.

The wind blew harder and colder, taunting me. I defied it by ignoring the pain in my back and stomach and not really caring if it got worse. I was going to finish what I started and it didn't matter who else knew I had done it. Tears froze on my face along with the sleet. I was crying for my mother, myself, and for Lori.

Why, God? I begged. *Why can't you just make it a little easier for us to get through this? Throughout my life, I have asked for help and direction. From a little child I was taught, "Ask and it shall be given to you." Even then I knew not to ask for foolish things. Requesting a new toy, a new bicycle, or a larger house never crossed my mind. No, I pleaded for important things, things that would help me lead a better, more dedicated life.*

"Ask and it shall be given to you!" the Bible says.

I asked for patience, and I received seven years of torture, starvation and cruelty at the hands of an abusive husband.

I asked for perseverance, and illness and death

entered my life, taking away some of those I loved most.

I asked for purpose, and I got a horrible disease that makes some people taunt me, call me a vampire.

I asked for a blessing, and I received a little girl, only to have her get the same terrible disease with which I suffer.

I asked to be beneficial to my husband, and I have legs that do not walk, arms that cannot hold, eyes that can never see the light of day, skin blistered so often that I cannot enjoy the touch of his passion.

Only the wind, blowing with even more fury, answered me as I walked on mile after mile.

The sun was going down—my tormentor rested.

Sharon pulled the car up beside me once more. She looked like she had been crying, too. "I just talked with Sheriff Alcott on the cellular phone. He says you're about a mile away." She had to yell for me to hear her through the wind. I had been so busy feeling sorry for myself that I hadn't even noticed the lights of the city in the distance.

"Is he going to give us an escort into town?" I asked.

"See that blue building up there? He'll be waiting in the parking lot for you. I told him it would be another twenty minutes or so." She was shielding her face from the sleet.

I looked in the back seat at Lori who was sound asleep. "You'd better wake her up! She wouldn't want to miss the police escort."

"I'll have her videotape the whole thing!" she replied.

"Tammy?"

"What?"

"I'm sorry. I should never have asked you to cheat." She started to cry again.

We hugged each other through the open car window.

"I'm sorry, too. You don't deserve to be the recipient of my frustration. I know you were just trying to help."

Sharon looked down at my feet. "Oh my God!"

That was another thing I hadn't paid much attention to in my anger. The padded mole skin I had inserted for comfort was hanging halfway out of my boot, covered with blood. Carefully, I stuffed it back inside. "I'll keep it on to protect them." Porphyria, like diabetes, makes the feet vulnerable to wounds.

Sharon said nothing. We had spoken enough harsh words to each other already.

I kept myself focused on the blue building in the distance as it got larger and larger. When I finally made it to the parking lot, the sheriff was standing by his car, holding onto his campaign hat in the wind.

"I'm Sheriff Alcott," he said, and shook my hand. "Can't believe this weather!"

"How much farther is it?" I yelled.

"Oh, I'd say about another quarter mile around that bend. That'll bring you to the city limits. The Holiday Inn that your friend said you're staying at is just a few blocks after that."

I was walking in place as we talked, trying to keep the circulation going in my legs and feet. "You're so good to help us," I said.

"It's my pleasure. I'm going to pull my vehicle out to the center lane. You just walk right behind me all the way to the motel. I won't drive too far ahead so I can keep an eye on you. Are you ready?"

I looked back at Sharon's car. Lori held the camera up as she waved me on. "Looks like we're all set. Let's move out!"

As I walked, I could feel my back paining me with each step. It was not the time to stop. I had to keep going, no matter how badly my body hurt.

I followed the sheriff through the traffic signals. The cars stopped on either side, waiting for me to pass through. Looking at the unknown faces inside the vans, trucks and cars, I expected them to be angry with me for interrupting their progress. But they weren't! Even though none of them had any idea what I was doing, they must have felt the excitement. They waved and called out, celebrating with me, not knowing why I was walking, but knowing that they could say that they had witnessed the unusual event.

A block ahead the neon green Holiday Inn sign beckoned me. Sheriff Alcott swerved his car around to barricade the oncoming traffic, giving me ample space to cross the road safely. He stepped out of his car, leaving his bubble lights on as he held his arms up in front of the traffic. My day had been filled with both emotional and physical torture. His kind gesture made everything feel a little less painful and a lot more meaningful. I walked toward him. His smile warmed my soul. "Thank you!" I called out.

At the front entrance to the motel, I found a dry spot and sat down to catch my breath. Sheriff Alcott came over. Sharon shut off the car and she and Lori joined me.

"Mom, are you okay?" Lori asked.

I nodded. "Sheriff Alcott, this is my daughter, Lori, and my friend, Sharon Bruce."

He shook their hands. "I'm pleased to meet both of you lovely young ladies. Are you keeping Tammy company?" he asked.

"We've tried," Sharon started to explain. "Let's just

say that Tammy has been doing a fine job out there." As she patted me on the back, I tried not to cry out.

"Well, I think it's real good of you to be traveling with her like this. Now, let's get you gals settled in your room so you can freshen up." Before taking his leave, he signed our sweatshirts with the white paint marker, thanking us for the opportunity to be part of the Trek.

In the room, I sat down on the edge of the bed, absolutely exhausted.

I walked into the bathroom and turned on the shower. The warm water soothed my aching body with all its unsightly bumps and bruises. Afterward, I slipped into bed and fell into a deep and dreamless sleep.

Chapter 23

R&R Time

As on all the other days, I awoke near dawn wanting to get an early start. Soon we were ready to begin. Hour after hour I hiked. Lori still wasn't well enough to join me. We were getting close to Boyne Mountain, the most luxurious place we would be staying on our journey. It was one of Michigan's largest ski resorts. There was no actual town, yet thousands of people visited the picturesque setting which provided all kinds of amenities necessary for a fun-filled get-away. The resort had donated a night's stay to us on this, the final night of our trek.

Just as we approached the entrance, I saw in the distance what appeared to be a full-sized van coming toward us on the road. We waited before turning into the driveway to see if the driver would acknowledge our existence. Sharon and Lori began waving. Sure enough, as the vehicle came closer into view, it slowed down just enough for us to see the driver and his passenger waving back. They even beeped their horn. For seven hours we had come in contact with nothing except long tractor trailers that would have preferred to run us down rather than look at us. Now, at the end of the day's journey, two kind souls had taken the time to notice us. We laughed hysterically as they went by, feeling like we had really accomplished something.

Soon we were registered and a uniformed bellman walked us to our villa. "Wow!" Lori's eyes widened to the size of saucers as he unlocked the door and she walked inside. Suddenly she called out, "I'm dead! I just know I am!"

"What are you talking about?" I asked as Sharon and I followed her in. Was Lori delirious?

"Yup! I am definitely dead!" she repeated, plopping herself on the sectional sofa in front of the massive stone fireplace. She put her feet up on the glass-topped coffee table and leaned back into a pile of plush decorator pillows. "I must have died somewhere out there on the road! It's the only explanation for why I have been rewarded by going to heaven. It's heaven, Mom! So I am most definitely dead!"

"No, my dear. You aren't quite dead yet." I sat down beside her. "But if you don't get your feet off that table, I'll oblige you!"

Lori got up from the sofa, half walking, half limping around the room. She looked like a little kid in a candy store, going from suite to suite, unable to resist touching it all. "What's behind this door?" She opened it and squealed, "It's another giant room with a queen-size bed and its own gorgeous bathroom." I walked to her side. In the corner was yet another fireplace. Next to it were a television and a stereo. I could hear her going through the rest of the rooms muttering, "Oh m'gosh! Oh m'gosh!" every few seconds. When she came back through the door, her arms were loaded down with a basket filled with goodies. "I just have to have that room, Mom! Please, can I have it? I promise I'll be good for the rest of my life if you'll just let me have that room!" I'd never seen her more excited.

"I'm not saying yes to anything until I've seen the other one."

"Come on," Lori called. I dragged my tattered feet across the floor to the other bedroom. Lori's eyes grew wide again. "I was wrong! We've all died and gone to heaven!" This bedroom was nearly identical to the other one, only with two queen-size beds instead of one. "Now can I have the first one, Mom?"

"Yes, go ahead!" It gave me such a good feeling to see my daughter so happy after her episode of illness.

I went back to the living room to look for Sharon. She had come in with us when we arrived, but I hadn't seen her since. I followed what sounded like her voice coming from the dining room. When I walked in, I found her on the telephone. My briefcase was on the table, its contents strewn all over.

"Yes, I'll hold," she said. Sharon covered the receiver. "I hope you don't mind. I had to find your address book. Don't worry. I'll clean up as soon as I'm done."

"Who are you talking to?" I asked.

"I'm on the phone with the television station in Traverse City. One way or another, they're going to interview you tomorrow!" I could hear the voice on the other end come back on. "Hello. Nancy? This is Sharon Bruce. Are you planning on covering the Trek for Truth?" Sharon paused. I watched the expression on her face turn from pleasantly hopeful to more than a little agitated. "Look, she's been

walking for six days! Maybe healthy people have no trouble
walking one hundred miles, but people who have this illness
can barely walk a block, and Tammy's been in the midst of
an attack. Now, I'm sure all of the people who have driven
by us are curious as to what she's doing out there. It would
be a shame if you were the only television station in all of
northern Michigan that didn't take the time to do a story on
the trek!"

My mouth dropped open. "Sharon!"

She cupped her hand over the receiver again. "Let me
handle this! If you can't be quiet, go in Lori's room and see
how she is." Sharon waved me off. "Yes, I'm still here. You'll
send a reporter out tomorrow morning? That's wonderful,
Nancy! Did you get the information I sent about porphyria?
Great! We'll be seeing you tomorrow then. What's that? Why,
that's very nice of you. I'll be sure to pass that on to Tammy.
Bye now." Sharon hung up the phone and reclined back in the
chair, her hands folded behind her head in satisfaction.

"I cannot believe what I just heard!"

"Wait a minute, Tammy! If you think about it, I did-
n't say one thing to her that wasn't true. There are only four
television stations in the entire area. Right?"

"Well, yes, but. . . ."

"The other three covered the opening ceremonies at
the beginning of the trek, or some facet of your work with the
association. If the Traverse City station didn't come out and
do a story on you, they would be the only ones who had
missed it!"

"I guess you're right. I had almost forgotten about the
media at the opening ceremony." It seemed so long ago that we
had been in that room filled with people who believed in us.

"Nancy wanted me to tell you that she wished you luck and she would be praying for you," Sharon said.

"That was nice. Is she the one who will be doing the interview?" I asked.

"She's going to send out one of the field reporters for that," she said. "Why don't you go and relax a little? I'm going to call home and let them know how we're doing. After that, we can have some supper." She hurried me out of the room, like she wanted some privacy. I thought it was kind of strange. Sharon had never seemed to mind before when I was in the room when she talked to her family. Nevertheless, I went along with it.

In the bathroom, I ran a wet washcloth over my face, feeling invigorated by the coolness against my blistered skin. I looked intently at the woman in the mirror staring back at me. She appeared exhausted. The lines of her forehead had grown deeper and longer than they were just a short time before, making her seem much older than she actually was. Half moons of grayish black underlined her reddened eyes and her skin was as pale as a ghost. It was almost too much to accept that I was looking at myself, that I was the one in the mirror that looked so old and worn.

For a few moments I stood there feeling sorry for myself and a few tears fell. Then I suddenly felt my tension ease. When I looked back again, I saw something else, something I had never seen in my face before. It was the look of calm maturity, the one that my grandmother had. The lines, the wrinkles, the eerie whiteness suddenly took on an entirely different character. I knew in my heart each one stood on its own merit, each one carrying great significance of important lessons. They deserved my respect and admiration, not self-pity or shame. I smiled at the person I'd become and headed back into the world.

Walking into the dining room, I heard Sharon still on the phone. She wasn't talking to her husband Mike, though. I heard her say Tim's name.

"I just wanted to make sure you were going to be there early when we came into Petoskey. She's in pretty bad shape, Tim. Tammy's going to need to see you and the kids when she comes over that last hill. I don't know if she should complete the walk. Her skin is blistered, her back and stomach trouble her so much I hear her groaning during the night. She's been trying to hide it, but I could tell she was having a lot of pain. I made sure she kept the sugar going all day. Oh, Tim, don't let on that we talked when she calls you tonight. I don't want her to know. She needs nothing but positive vibes to build up her spirits. Will you call Mike and let him know what time to be there? All right, then, we'll see you tomorrow. Bye."

I held onto the back of the door, feeling tears starting to well up in my eyes again. Sharon was running the gauntlet for me, making sure there would be love and encouragement so I could make it to the end. I slipped back into the bathroom so she wouldn't find me standing by the door listening.

A few moments later she poked her head into the bathroom. "You about ready? I'm starving!"

"I'll be right out," I said, giving her a smile.

Later that night I called Tim, keeping the conversation I had overheard earlier a secret. He asked me how I was feeling and I told him fine. I talked to my children, telling each one how much I loved them. They sounded excited that we would be back together the next day. We kept the conversation light on both ends. There would be time after the trek was over to discuss my disease and gory details with my husband.

Tim promised he would be in the parking lot with the children when I arrived. We had planned it that way from the beginning. We all would walk the last mile of the Trek for Truth together. Sharon knew that, too. I think it just made her feel good to make sure everything ran as smoothly as possible for the last day of this fight for our cause. Tim and I didn't talk about porphyria. We didn't discuss pain or those we'd met who hadn't cared. There was only room for the good parts and an "I love you" and an "I miss you." We put aside all of the horrible things that porphyria had brought into our lives, spending a few moments talking about good things and our happiness.

Afterwards, Lori and I spent some quiet time writing in our journals while Sharon soaked in the whirlpool. I reflected on the journey and recorded my personal feelings and my dreams for my own and Lori's futures.

I glanced over at my daughter engrossed in her writing wondering what she was saying about our trek. She looked so tired and yet tranquil and more mature than before we left home. As I watched her, my love for her grew.

On this journey we had become bound together by more than our blood ties. Porphyria had made us sisters in a way neither of us could have ever foreseen.

Chapter 24

Closer and Closer

Soft colors blended in the sky harmoniously above the large golden ball rising in the east. I watched the horizon early and then turned away from the approaching sun, as I've always had to. The fresh breeze swirled around the branches of the snow-etched pine trees, rustling their dark green needles and making a kind of music. Listening, I took a deep, strengthening breath. Then I went back inside our villa.

My stomach churned and flip-flopped. I couldn't tell if it was the porphyria acting up, or the excitement. Either way, I grabbed a bottle of orange juice from the refrigerator and gulped it down. It would be wise for Lori and me to take in as many carbohydrates as possible before starting again on our way.

"Time to wake up, sweetheart," I whispered to my sleeping child. "Only one more day to go!"

She rolled over toward me with a look of anguish on her face. "I don't feel good again, Mom. My back hurts."

I sat down beside her on the bed and began rubbing

out the knots of pain. "I brought you a juice. Here, sit up and take a sip. It will help you feel better."

Lori propped her back against the pillows and tried to wake up enough to take a drink. "What time is it? It looks like it's still dark outside."

"It's six o'clock. We have to get going if we're going to make it to Petoskey on time," I said.

"Gosh, Mom! I feel sick again." She tried to roll over and go back to sleep.

"No, no, dearest. If I can do it, you can do it." I turned on my marching music and marched in place beside her bed.

Her eyes lit up just the littlest bit at the sight of me and the elevator music sound. I held up the tape deck. "Should I keep it on?"

Lori sat up straight in the bed and took the bottle of juice from my hand. She started sipping. "No. Whatever you do, no more of that music. Just give me a while to wake up a little more."

"Lori." I was suddenly serious. "I don't want you to push yourself too far."

She nodded. "Mom, I want to be with you, but I don't know if I can do it."

"Lori, you must only do what you comfortably can. That's part of accepting this illness. Having you walk beside me has meant so much. What you can do for me and our cause now is to get better so that we can support each other. I'll wake up Sharon now."

I walked into the other room quietly, hoping to surprise Sharon. As I stepped around the door, I saw that the covers were thrown back and she wasn't there.

"Looking for something?" she shouted behind me.

"Good Lord, Sharon! You scared me." My heart pounded as she giggled with the delight of sneaking up on me. "What are you doing up and dressed already?"

"I don't know," she said. "I guess I was just too excited to sleep. I heard you when you went outside before dawn, so I decided I should be up, too. Is Lori awake yet?"

"She's up, but I'm not sure she's really well enough to walk. Her back hurts so much." I looked away with tears in my eyes and stared out the window for a moment. Just past the golf course I caught a glimpse of the road we would be traveling that day. It was waiting for me to finish what I had begun. I turned to Sharon. "Let's get started," I said.

I hobbled around the villa, packing up some things. Lori was limping and still pale. "Lori, don't feel badly, but you must ride in the car," I said, taking the decision out of her hands.

"Thanks, Mom," she said nodding. Packing the car was sad, as none of us wanted to leave. We rode past the lodge, the ski slopes, and the golf course, soaking in as much of the resort as we could before turning onto the main road. "We'll have to come back here again someday," I said.

"Yes!" Lori agreed with me. "But next time, we're going to drive!"

Sharon pulled the car up to the large, green mileage sign just a few hundred yards up the road. Each of us posed for a photo beneath it, pointing to the words *Petoskey: twenty miles*.

Blowing a kiss to Lori, I began walking. By eight o'clock, the traffic began to pick up. We would have a lot more than small trucks to keep us company on this part of U.S. 131 that led into the city. People were driving to work. Many that passed us slowed down when they saw the red flashing light on top of the car. They beeped their horns and waved as they passed. From the car Lori waved back to each one. Perhaps, I thought, people knew we were coming. The word might have spread around the hospital and clinic. Maybe, I fantasized, the cars that passed by were filled with people who worked there and they wanted to support us.

"Tammy! Look!" Sharon yelled out the window of the car. She pointed to the bottom of the hill. There was a small blue van parked on the opposite side of the road. The man standing next to it had a video camera held up to his face. He was taping our approach. As I got closer, I could vaguely make out the television station logo on the side of the car.

The reporter waited there. I walked toward him and he taped every step that I took. I felt nervous, even though I was happy we were going to get publicity.

"Hi," he said, "I'm Jeff."

I shook his hand, slowing down only a little. "And I'm Tammy. If you don't mind, I'd like to keep going while we talk. I'm afraid if I slow down I won't make it up that next hill."

He nodded, laughing at my comment. We were both feeling a little more at ease now. "I have all the information on your disease back at the office, so I guess I'll start with some questions about the trek itself." He held the camera back up to his face and pressed the record button. "Now, tell me, Tammy. Do you think you have accomplished what you set out to do? Were you really able to educate people about porphyria?"

I thought maybe he would start out with something simple like, *How has the weather been for you the past seven days?* But no! He started the interview off with a biggie! I took a few moments to think about how I would answer his question.

Then I said, "I would have to say that each person who's been willing to listen has learned a little about porphyria. We passed out our information pamphlets at every place we stopped. A lot of people were willing to wear our purple ribbons. That's really how the education will spread. Others will ask what the ribbons stand for, and it will give the person wearing the ribbon a chance to tell what he or she learned."

"How have you been feeling physically along the way? Any signs that this has affected your disease?"

"I have some symptoms of porphyria every day of my life and, under the stress of the trek, some have increased. Walking was sometimes very difficult, but that's not what's important. I had to do it and now I feel satisfied that I have."

He clicked off the camera and smiled at me. "That's great, Tammy! I'm going to run back to my car and catch up with you at the base of the next hill."

Before I could say anything else, he was gone.

At the base of the next hill he took more pictures. "Well," he said, "that's, as we say in my business, a wrap."

I thanked him for his time and continued on my way. But when I looked back I saw him taping Lori waving to him as the car rolled away and over the crest of the hill. Lori was smiling.

We had gone just over seventeen miles. The afternoon sun was shining brightly in the sky. Too bright, in fact. I removed the heavy cotton turtleneck from underneath my sweatshirt. I was taking a risk exposing my neck to the sun, but the temperature was rising to an unbearable level. The heat and the porphyria had me backed into a corner. Whatever choice I made, I was going to be uncomfortable. There was no way to avoid it.

My feet were beginning to swell even more now and the throbbing in my back had returned. The sticky adhesive of the mole skin I'd applied pulled at the torn skin of my feet making them burn and itch. Still, I had to go on. There were only a couple more miles. If I could make it to the mall parking lot, the rest would be easy. All three of us would be walking the last mile. The triumph would be worth it, no matter what condition my body was in at the end.

In the distance I made out the shape of the silvery blue Petoskey water tower. It stood at the top of a hill right in the center of town near the shore of Little Traverse Bay. I focused on the hazy image, walking as steadily as I could toward it. My feet burned beneath me, and I felt wobbly.

Lori got out of the car and limped towards me, "Here, Mom," she said, handing me a juice bottle with a straw in it. She could see that I was becoming weaker from the heat and the pain. "Maybe you should get in the car and rest a while."

"No, Lori. I have to do this. I have to be able to look back on this someday and know that I finished."

"Mrs. Bruce told me you would say that and to not even bother asking you to stop," she said. "I accept that you have to go on, but please keep drinking the juice. If you need another, just hold up the empty bottle and I'll bring one to you." She kissed me on the cheek and limped back to the car.

I sighed. I was alone now and would be until I reached the parking lot where everyone would be waiting. There would be a lot of excitement, a time of celebration as we met our families and prepared for the last mile to the clinic. That part of it was for Sharon, Lori and me to relish. Before I got to that point, I needed the time to reflect privately.

I replayed the scenes of these days in my mind. The people I had met, the places I had been, they had all become a special part of me. Had I accomplished all that I had hoped I would? It wasn't so much a question of accomplishment anymore. When I planned the Trek for Truth, it had been my intention to be the messenger, the teacher of an important lesson. As I remembered each of the kind souls who had taken the time to give me a piece of themselves to carry with me, I realized that I was the one who had learned the greatest lesson of all.

They had taught me to open my heart to strangers. With each hand that had been extended to me, with every arm wrapped around my shoulder and kind word, a piece of my protective wall and fear of rejection had crumbled away.

Coming through all the storms, both physical and emotional, meeting those who had encouraged and even those who had rejected my message, I learned to face my fears. The trek had taught me that, no matter what, I didn't have to be afraid anymore to let people see and know porphyria. I didn't have to hide my face any longer or my suffering from those I met. Most of all, I no longer had to be afraid of who I was, how I looked and what I stood for. Nor did I always have to be strong. Sometimes, it was better to accept the weakness inside of me, so others could be the strong ones and carry the load when it was too heavy to bear. There were going to be times in my life, such as now, when doing it all by myself was the right way, the only way. Nevertheless it was a comfort to finally realize that I didn't have to be alone if I didn't want to be. When my spirit felt the despair of darkness and desolation, all I had to do was find the courage to reach out my hand and my heart.

Though I was experiencing pain, I stood erect and adjusted my dark glasses so I could see in the daylight. The final moments of aloneness were here. Just ten feet away stood my family, applauding and cheering. I walked to them proudly and then collapsed into the open arms of my husband, melting into his welcoming embrace. The children and he gathered around me. Lori joined us.

"I knew you could do it, hon. I'm so proud of you!" Tim steadied my trembling arms, leading me and the children to a shady spot underneath a tree at the edge of the parking lot. "And of you, Lori." He embraced our daughter.

Lori, Reuben, Dan and Johanna sat down next to me underneath the tree, chattering away about how happy I looked when I saw them. It was so good to hear the sounds of their voices, even if they were all running together in my head. I searched for Sharon, who had disappeared, wondering where she had wandered off to. Looking past the faces of my children, I saw her. She was sitting under another tree with one arm around her son, Rob, and the other around her husband Mike. They were enjoying their own moment of silent reflection and private celebration.

"You made it, Mom!" Dan reached his hand out to give mine a special squeeze hug. "How does it feel?"

"It feels really good, but I'm a little shaky." I looked down at my feet. The laces had come undone, and the hiking shoes, though they were larger than my regular size, felt tighter than they had that morning. My feet had swollen even more, if that was possible. I lifted my pant legs to see why my ankles hurt so bad. As I did, I saw that they had swollen too, bulging over the rims of my socks.

I sipped on the bottle of water Tim handed me. It felt so good to rest. Looking up, I saw a man in a blue uniform. "Are you the woman who's walking the Trek for Truth?" he asked, in a deep authoritative voice. It was the Michigan state trooper who was going to escort us the last mile.

"Why yes, I am." I smiled at him. "Is it time for us to get going?" I started to get up.

"We can't leave now, Mom!" Lori got a panicky look on her face. "Grandma and Grandpa aren't here yet!"

"That's right. I almost forget that they were coming. You don't mind if we wait a little while longer, do you?" I asked the trooper. "We can't leave without my parents."

"Not a problem," he said.

Mom and Dad pulled into the parking lot about five minutes later. They got out of their car and walked over to us, carrying three small silver boxes. My mother opened one of the boxes, taking out a beautiful white rose corsage framed with our signature purple ribbon. As she surveyed my weak condition, she bent towards me. With tears in her eyes, she pinned the corsage to my sweatshirt, whispering in my ear as she hugged me, "I love you, Tam." She did the same with Lori and Sharon.

Dad was getting ready to videotape the end of our journey, while Mom went to the others in our bunch, making sure each of them had a purple ribbon. After Dad fiddled and fumbled with the camera for a while, and everyone was spit-shined to Mother's satisfaction, it was time to start reassembling.

Dad ran up to the top of that final hill to capture our approach. The state trooper took his place in front of us, then

Tim and the children in his car, and Mike followed in
Sharon's car at the rear. The trooper sounded the siren. He
and Mike turned on their cars' bubble lights, signaling that it
was time for everyone else to take their places.

Sharon walked over to me. "This is it! The moment
you've been dreaming about! Give me your hand."

I held it out to her and she clasped it in her own.
Sharon pulled me up and I steadied my trembling body
against the tree for a moment. Pain instantly shot through my
legs and back again, but I found my balance. We walked over
to join Lori and we all took our places at the head of the line.
"Give me your hand," I repeated Sharon's words to Lori. The
three of us stood there, hand in hand. We were finally ready
to walk the last leg of our journey.

The state police car moved slowly up the ramp that led
to the main road as we followed behind. My heart began to
pound inside my chest, not from illness or fear, but from the
exhilaration of the moment. The excitement rushed through
me, filling my being with its energizing power. I could sense
us becoming stronger with every step we took. As we turned
the corner onto the road, I felt my feet become lighter, gliding
across the pavement.

We made our way down the busy street between the
lines of traffic on either side. We had succeeded in our
journey across the state. We had succeeded in dragging
porphyria out of the secret place in which it often lies hidden. We had laid the groundwork. I knew it was just a
beginning, but for the three of us and others it was an
important one. One that would lead to our real Trek for
Truth in the future.

As we approached the massive brick buildings of the

clinic and hospital complex, I saw Janeene Taylor, the reporter who'd done the first news story about porphyria, racing from her parked car to catch our arrival. She pulled a camera from her bag, snapping photographs at a furious pace. Slowly, we walked toward her, and toward the big blue arch that was now just a few feet away. I could see a crowd, both familiar and unfamiliar faces, gathered at the entrance of the clinic, waiting to share that final moment with us.

I held tightly to Sharon's and Lori's hands on either side of me and raised them along with mine high above our heads.

Epilogue

I reached over Tim to grab the telephone so its ringing wouldn't wake him up. It was Saturday morning, our only day of the week to catch up on our sleep.

"Mrs. Evans? Is this Mrs. Tammy Evans?"

In my hazy state, I tried to make out the voice on the other end. It was a man's voice, deep and sad, with a hint of urgency in it. I rubbed my eyes and focused on the numbers on the alarm clock. It was only seven o'clock. "Yes, this is Tammy Evans. May I ask who's calling?" I said, trying to prop myself up in bed.

"I hope I didn't wake you. My name is Bill Jenkins, Mrs. Evans. I served in the Gulf War and it made me very ill, Mrs. Evans." It was obvious he was upset.

"Oh, that's all right. And, please, call me Tammy."

He stumbled on. "I'm calling because I saw you on TV and I think I have porphyria." He could barely get the words out. "The lady at a motel in Atlanta gave me your telephone number. I hope that's all right."

"Yes, it's definitely okay," I said. Since arriving home from the trek, I had begun to receive some alarming articles on the mysterious symptoms affecting Gulf War veterans and the possible relation to porphyria. This relationship had been strongly substantiated by the research of a Dr. Donnay at a clinic Specializing in Multiple Chemical Sensitivity (MCS) disorder. The articles made me remember the ignorance of the reporter who had told me not enough people were dying of the disease for the media to be interested.

My information came mostly from medical abstracts by physicians in other countries or websites for a popular vampire role-playing game called "Porphyria." One was different, though. It was information for veterans of Desert Storm. More precisely, it was a resource for those suffering from Gulf War Syndrome.

Albert Donnay, MRR Executive Director, believes that most Persian Gulf veterans with unexplained illness also will be shown to have one or more types of porphyria, and most likely Intoxication Porphyria (IP). IP is the only type associated with multiple enzyme deficiencies, although it may not be the only acquired (non-inherited) form of the disease. At least one form known to be inherited, Porphyria Cutanea Tarda (PCT), has developed in individuals without any inherited porphyria-specific enzyme deficiencies after they were exposed to particular chemicals such as hexachlorobenzene. The inherited types of porphyria also may prove significant, however, especially in those cases in which the children of Persian Gulf veterans have begun to display similar symptoms.

Never in my wildest dreams had I expected my search for answers about my illness to unfold such a startling revelation. I remembered reading on.

Unlike the more controversial diagnosis of MCS, which the VA refuses to accept, VA officials cannot claim ignorance of porphyria. The VA agreed in July 1993 to a recommendation to compensate Vietnam Veterans suffering from PCT. While this recommendation was based solely on a literature review, the VA has since checked for and found 100 cases of porphyria reported in its Agent Orange Registry. Although this is already several times the expected rate, the actual rate is undoubtedly much higher, since the Registry's medical examinations—like that developed for Persian Gulf veterans—still does not recommend any specific medical history question or diagnostic tests for porphyria.

This doctor was saying that there was scientific evidence that the Gulf War mystery illness was really porphyria! He was also saying that the United States government had known about porphyria all along. The Veterans' Administration was even compensating Vietnam veterans for contracting my disease from exposure to Agent Orange!

Suddenly, as Bill continued talking, I realized that my prayer to God for guidance during the trek had been answered. For a moment, I prayed, *Lord, forgive me. Now I know that when I angrily asked you, why me, you wanted me to understand if not me, then who?*

I refocused on Bill. "Are you having an attack of porphyria now, Bill?" I asked.

"Yes. I think so." His voice trembled as he told me his symptoms. I recognized the familiar signs.

"The pain, the nausea, not being able to go out in the sun, the anxiety of not knowing if I will ever be well again. It's so frightening to me and my family. I've been to so many doctors. Recently, I read about the work of Dr. Donnay on us veterans and porphyria, and I just knew. I just knew I had it. Then I saw you on television, and I had," he broke down again, "to call," he said.

"Bill, I want you to calm down," I addressed him in an authoritative tone. "You're only going to make yourself sicker if you panic."

"I'm sorry." His voice grew calmer. "This is all just so much to take in at one time."

"Is there someone with you, Bill? Do you have somebody who can look after you?" I asked.

"Yes, my wife is here, and my sister is planning to stay with me this afternoon after my wife goes to work."

"Good. The first thing you have to do is to be tested. Do you know where to go?"

"I don't know anything. That's the problem."

"Well, first you must go to a doctor who can test for the disease. I'll give you some names." I recited the names of a few doctors and clinics and paused while he wrote them down.

He promised that he would. "All I want to do is feel better!" His voice broke again. "It just seems like there's no hope, like there's no one I can turn to who will understand what I'm going through."

"I understand, Bill." I attempted to reassure him. "I'm

going to help you as much as I can. But what you have to understand is that not much is known and that in the end you are going to have to reach deep within yourself for the strength to fight this disease."

I began to talk to him about raising his sugar intake. I explained to him what carbohydrate therapy was all about and how it could make him feel better. "Bill, before you try out any of my suggestions, I want you to call some of the doctors I named. See one and find out if you have it and what you can do to decrease your pain."

"Right now I feel so alone, despite my wife and friends. Do you think it would be possible for us to meet? Could you come to my house so we could talk some more? I'd really appreciate it if you could. I feel too sick to go out." He was sounding desperate again.

"I'll tell you what." I took my date book out of my purse on the nightstand to check my schedule. "I can be there tomorrow afternoon. How's one o'clock sound to you?"

"Oh, Tammy! That would just be wonderful. Thank you so much!"

We talked a little while longer and, as we did, I reflected on how sick and alone I had once felt. I thought about the day the doctor had finally given a name to my agony.

"Bill, I know just what you're feeling. Not so long ago those feelings were mine. I want you to get some rest and don't forget to call the doctor. I'll be there tomorrow. And, Bill, one more thing."

"What's that, Tammy?"

"More than anything else, I want you to remember this. I'm here for you. Day or night you can call me if you're frightened or just want to talk. I won't let you face porphyria by yourself. I promise you, Bill, you will never be alone again!"

Appendix A

Porphyria Testing Suggested
For Gulf War Veterans

by Albert Donnay

A rare but well known condition might hold the answer for victims of the mysterious Persian Gulf Syndrome. MCS Referral & Resources (MRR) announced at the November meeting of the Persian Gulf Experts Scientific Committee that all of the diverse neurological, dermatological, and psychological symptoms being seen in Persian Gulf veterans with supposedly "unexplained" illness might be caused by one or more types of porphyria.

These rare but well established medical conditions apparently have not been considered as a possible explanation for Persian Gulf Syndrome by the Department of Defense (DOD) or Veterans' Affairs (VA) or any of the expert panels convened to date—all of which so far have failed to come up with a diagnosis or even a case definition.

The porphyrias are a group of mostly inherited and incurable enzyme deficiency disorders which are aggravated by exposure to chemicals, drugs, other environmental and physiological stressors. As documented in over 300 peer reviewed articles* spanning more than 100 years of research, symptoms of porphyria depend on which enzyme deficiency is involved and may include any combination of multiple chemical sensitivity (MCS) [evidenced by intolerance of chemical odors]; heavy metal sensitivity [evidenced by intolerance of dental amalgams and/or jewelry]; photosensitivity [evidenced by neurological and dermatological reactions to sunlight]; skin sensitivity [evidenced by diverse reactions to various stressors]; abdominal pains; muscle and joint pains; chronic fatigue; neuropsychological complaints; and dark, pink or red urine.

MRR urged the DOD and VA to immediately begin asking about and recording these symptoms of porphyria in their Persian Gulf Registry examinations. Any patient reporting even a few of these symptoms should promptly be given the very specific laboratory tests by the Mayo Clinic and others to detect and distinguish among the various forms of porphyria. These tests include twenty-four hour urine and stool porphyrins, fractionated; total red blood cell porphyrins, fractionated; and the four red blood cell porphyrin enzymes which are needed to detect specific enzyme deficiencies.

Independent physicians who began using these tests with civilian MCS patients earlier this year report that more than 60% of their patients are testing positive for one or more types of porphyria.

Albert Donnay, MRR Executive Director, believes that most Persian Gulf veterans with "unexplained illness" also will be shown to have one or more types of porphyria, and most likely Intoxication Porphyria(IP). IP is the only type associated with multiple enzyme deficiencies, although it may not be the only acquired (non-inherited) form of the disease. At least one form known to be inherited, Porphyria Cutanea Tarda (PCT), has developed in individuals without any inherited porphyria-specific enzyme deficiencies after they were exposed to particular chemicals such as hexachlorobenzene. The inherited types of porphyria also may prove significant, however, especially in those cases in which the children of Persian Gulf veterans have begun to display similar symptoms.

While there is no cure for porphyria, those with the disease—like those with MCS—should be counseled to avoid aggravating exposures to sunlight, heavy metals, and chemicals (especially unnecessary medications.)

Unlike the more controversial diagnosis of MCS, which the VA refuses to accept, VA officials cannot claim ignorance of porphyria. The VA agreed in July 1993 to a recommendation to compensate Vietnam Veterans suffering from PCT. While this recommendation was based solely on a literature review, the VA has since checked for and found 100 cases of porphyria reported in its Agent Orange Registry (equivalent to 71 per 100,000). Although this is already several times the expected rate, the actual rate is undoubtedly much higher, since the Registry's medical examinations—like that developed for Persian Gulf veterans—still does not recommend any specific medical history questions or diagnostic tests for porphyria.

* The National Library of Medicine and the National Cancer Institute lists over 6,000 articles on the subject of porphyria since these databases were first set up in 1966.

Editor's Note: Any doctor can order the tests listed in this article. The phone number for the Mayo Clinic Laboratory is (800) 533-1710. Porphyria is also being found in patients suffering from silicone implant and chronic fatigue syndromes.

A list of porphyrinogenic chemicals and drugs may be obtained from CIIN, PO Box 301, White Sulphur Springs, MT 59645; EARN, PO Box 426, Williston, ND 58802; or MRR, 2326 Pickwick Rd., Baltimore, MD 21207 by sending $1 plus SASE.

Appendix B

Gulf War Illnesses

U.S. soldiers in Gulf during war: 690,000.

Gulf soldiers with persistent illnesses: 63,000 veterans and active-duty U.S. soldiers. Of the 399,473 retired Gulf War soldiers, a total of 2550 are suffering from heart disease, 2356 from neurological disease and 3034 from respiratory disease. No accurate estimate is available for those suffering from various cancers. Scores of veterans and active-duty soldiers complain that their sicknesses have caused disease among spouses, and disease or deformities among babies and children. At least 2200 Gulf War veterans have died since the war. This estimate does not cover those who died while on active duty.

Civilians: An undetermined number of the 3000 U.S. civilians who worked in the Gulf during the war are sick.
Foreign soldiers/civilians: Hundreds of British, French, Czech, Saudi Arabian, Canadian, Norwegian, Kuwaiti and Austrian

troops, as well as thousands of Saudi Arabian, Kuwaiti and Iraqi civilians, have reported chronic illnesses with symptoms similar to those experienced by U.S. Gulf War veterans.

Symptoms: Respiratory and stomach illnesses, nerve damage, rashes, joint pain, short-term memory loss and stress.

Possible causes: Oil-well fires, insects, depleted uranium, chemical or biological weapons, vaccines and pills the soldiers were ordered to take.

SOURCES: U.S. Defense and Veterans Affairs departments, U.S. Senate Banking and Veterans committees, Gulf War veterans' advocates, civilians who served in the war, Iraqi News Service, U.S. and foreign press accounts.

From *The Hartford Courant*

Appendix C

Health Effects of Agent Orange

The staff of the National Information System for Vietnam Veterans and Their Families is often asked a most compelling question: Did my exposure to Agent Orange cause my child's health problems? To help families receive an answer to this question we have reviewed the scientific literature to find what many scientists who have studied this issue have concluded.

There is a lot of information available concerning Agent Orange and its effects. Yet, we are unable to provide a more complete discussion of this issue than the one found in *Veterans and Agent Orange: Health Effects of Herbicides Used in Vietnam*, a recent report by the Institute of Medicine's National Academy of Science. Because this report is considered the most comprehensive to date, we have extracted information from it and summarized it into this brief fact sheet.

According to Harold Fallen, Institute of Medicine Committee Chairperson, extreme views have evolved on the Agent Orange issue. One extreme is the view that Agent Orange causes a wide range of diseases, while the other is that exposure to Agent Orange has not led to any health problems. The committee determined, through an extensive review of the scientific literature, that there is a link between exposure to herbicides and certain diseases.

Most of the evidence the committee reviewed about adverse health effects came from studies of people who were exposed because of their jobs or from industrial accidents. These types of exposures were often at high levels and for long periods of time. Getting a clear picture of the health risks for Vietnam veterans is not so straightforward because the levels of exposure varied so much. While most veterans probably had lower exposure levels, some may have experienced levels as high as persons exposed in occupational or agricultural accidents. What is uncertain is how many veterans may have been exposed to those higher levels and who they are.

Committee Vice Chairperson David Tollerud said, "We simply do not know the degree of risk for Vietnam veterans. We do feel, however, that enough information exists to allow studies to be done that would lead to a better understanding of the risk that veterans face for contracting diseases related to herbicide exposure in Vietnam."

The committee's report specifically focuses on Agent Orange and other herbicides used in Vietnam, some of which contained dioxin, an unintended byproduct of the manufacturing process. They found evidence that links three cancers and two other illnesses with chemicals used in herbicides in the Vietnam War. Those diseases are soft tissue sarcoma, non-Hodgkin's lymphoma, and Hodgkin's disease, also the skin diseases chloracne and porphyria cutanea tarda (PCT). The committee also concluded that new studies that would piece together different types of information could help find how much the risk of disease is increased in veterans who were exposed to herbicides such as Agent Orange.

In determining whether a link existed between herbicides, or dioxin, and other health problems, the committee's conclusions fell into the following categories:

Sufficient Evidence of an Association: Evidence is sufficient to conclude that there is a positive association with the following conditions: soft tissue sarcoma, non-Hodgkin's lymphoma, Hodgkin's disease, chloracne, and porphyria cutanea tarda in genetically susceptible individuals.

Limited or Suggestive Evidence: The committee found limited or suggestive evidence of an association between exposure to herbicides of the kind used in Vietnam and three other cancers: respiratory cancers, prostate cancer, and multiple myeloma.

Inadequate Evidence: The scientific data for most cancers and other diseases, such as adverse neurological and reproductive effects, were inadequate or insufficient to decide whether an association exists with the following: birth defects, childhood cancer in offspring, infertility, testicular cancer, and female reproductive cancers.

No Association: For a small group of cancers, the committee found that a sufficient number and variety of well-designed studies exist to conclude that there is limited or suggestive evidence of no association between these cancers and the herbicides or dioxin. This group includes skin cancer, gastrointestinal tumors (colon, rectal, stomach, and pancreatic), bladder cancer, and brain tumors.

The committee found that exposure assessment was the

weakest element in most studies of veterans. While some studies show a link between adverse health effects and herbicides or dioxin, there is no reliable way of determining which individuals may have received high exposures during service in Vietnam. The report states that evidence about exposure during the war suggests that Vietnam veterans as a group had substantially lower exposure to herbicides and dioxins than the subjects in many occupational studies. Veterans who participated in Operation Ranch Hand are an exception to this pattern because of their direct involvement in spraying. In Operation Ranch Hand about 19 million gallons of herbicide were sprayed over 3.6 million acres of South Vietnam.

The report urged that a non-governmental organization be commissioned to develop and test new methods of evaluating herbicide exposure in Vietnam veterans. These new methods would draw on historical reconstructions and include information on the spraying that occurred around base camps and other areas that could have led to higher human exposures. Important information could be gained from historical records of ground and perimeter spraying, herbicide shipment to various military bases, and knowledge of the type of terrain and foliage typical of the locations sprayed and the military mission of the troops located there.

What this report means is that the answer to the question, of whether parents' exposure to Agent Orange caused their children's health problems, is still unknown. It is important to note that the report did not say that these problems were not caused by exposure. This leaves open the hope that an answer will eventually be found. For many years, veterans with soft tissue sarcoma, non-Hodgkin's lymphoma, Hodgkin's disease, and chloracne believed that there was a relationship and the report proved they were right.

As of the writing of this fact sheet the Veterans Administration has acknowledged the following conditions as service connected due to exposure to Agent Orange: chloracne, peripheral neuropathy, soft tissue sarcoma, non-Hodgkin's lymphoma, Hodgkin's disease, chloracne, multiple myeloma, respiratory cancers, and *porphyria cutanea tarda*.

Appendix D

Intoxication Porphyria

This is a syndrome that develops when toxic chemicals or heavy metals interfere with the enzymes that metabolize the intermediates in the production of heme which makes hemoglobin for our red blood cells.

This is a new concept concerning the manner in which these environmental toxins can cause symptomatic illness. Some of the symptoms that may be experienced are:

Abdominal pain	Muscle weakness	Insomnia
Nausea	Sensory loss	Depression
Vomiting	Fine tremors	Sun sensitivity
Constipation	Restlessness	Disorientation
Tachycardia	Excess sweating	Hallucinations
Hypertension	Painful urination	Paranoia
Mental Symptoms	Anxiety	Skin lesions
Pain in limbs, neck, head, chest		

The evaluation requires blood, urine and stool studies for porphyrin metabolism. These studies can elucidate the reason for very difficult symptom complexes in the chronically ill patient.

The treatment depends on the severity of the symptoms, but the most important part of the therapy is to look for the causes and to remove them.

Porphyria
The Woman Who Has
"The Vampire Disease"
A True Story
Tammy Evans

* Without warning, the pain strikes; her complexion becomes eerily waxy, her skin sizzles in the sun, her eyes are blinded by daylight. She is subject to abrupt mood swings and acute visual distortion.

* This description seems to fit a character in a science fiction story, however, it is not fiction.

* Tammy Evans is afflicted with Porphyria, the sickness historically thought to have caused King George III's mad spells and labeled by lay people "The Vampire Disease."

* It is a strange and deadly illness now claimed by some noted researchers to cause, in one of its mutant forms, Gulf War Syndrome.

The real life horror of the Tammy Evans story lies not only in the bizarre details of porphyria's effects on the human body, the way it forces its victims away to hide from the sun and the way it renders them ghostly pale. It is evident in the all-too-plain cruelty she has to face from a society obsessed with appearance and a medical community unwilling to admit it can't cure some illnesses. This book is the moving story of Tammy's struggle to alert doctors to the dangers porphyria poses and to reveal to the public the silent sufferings of its often outcast victims, whose growing list now includes: Vietnam veterans and those facing Chronic Fatigue and Gulf War Syndrome.